RAND NATIONAL DEFENSE RESEARCH INSTITUTE



# U.S. Special Operations Forces in the Philippines, 2001–2014

Linda Robinson, Patrick B. Johnston, Gillian S. Oak

Prepared for the Office of the Assistant Secretary of Defense

For more information on this publication, visit www.rand.org/t/RR1236

Library of Congress Cataloging-in-Publication Data
is available for this publication.

ISBN: 978-0-8330-9210-6

Published by the RAND Corporation, Santa Monica, Calif.


*Cover Image: DoD photo by Mass Communication Specialist 1st Class Chris Fahey, U.S. Navy/Released*

# Preface

This report examines the role of U.S. special operations forces in Operation Enduring Freedom—Philippines from 2001 to 2014. The report documents the chief activities of U.S. special operations forces and their effects on transnational terrorist threats in the southern Philippines, the capacity and capability of the Philippine security forces, and the U.S.-Philippines bilateral relationship. The purpose of the report is to provide an authoritative and comprehensive account of a long-duration special operations mission to aid policymakers and military planners, as well as for use in professional military education. This detailed account illustrates the varied and robust types of operational assistance provided as a critical component of foreign internal defense, which distinguishes this special operations mission from security cooperation activities and train-and-equip missions. Foreign internal defense often includes training and equipping, but the focus is on employing and not just building capacity and capability. And unlike security cooperation, which often aims to secure access and build relationships, foreign internal defense seeks to harness those activities to achieve an operational result. To achieve that result, U.S. forces carry out a wide range of enabling and advisory activities on or near the battlefield, which can include direct support to combat or combat advising in accordance with rules of engagement established by U.S. policy and host-nation agreement, as well as civil affairs and information operations. Although the specific activities can vary, the U.S. emphasis in foreign internal defense is on supporting the objectives, plans, and operations of the host nation and partner forces.

This research was sponsored by the Office of the Assistant Secretary of Defense for Special Operations/Low-Intensity Conflict and conducted within the International Security and Defense Policy Center of the RAND National Defense Research Institute, a federally funded research and development center sponsored by the Office of the Secretary of Defense, the Joint Staff, the Unified Combatant Commands, the Navy, the Marine Corps, the defense agencies, and the defense Intelligence Community.

For more information on the RAND International Security and Defense Policy Center, see www.rand.org/nsrd/ndri/centers/isdp or contact the director (contact information is provided on the web page).

# Contents

# Figures

## Summary

The purpose of this report is to document the activities of U.S. special operations forces (SOF) in Operation Enduring Freedom—Philippines (OEF-P) and evaluate the outcomes to which they contributed. We designed this report for policymakers and military planners to use for future long-duration special operations missions and in professional military education. This report is the most comprehensive and authoritative account of OEF-P produced to date. No previous study has documented the entire 14 years of activities in detail and examines the evolution in the joint special operations task force's (JSOTF's) approach, its interaction with the U.S. country team, and the effects achieved in terms of the threat and threat environment, as well as the capability of Philippine Security Forces (PSF) and their approach to the southern Philippines.

In 2001, the U.S. government embarked on a 14-year effort to address transnational terrorist threats in the historically restive southern Philippines, where the majority of the country's Muslim population resides. During this time, a JSOTF commanded a continuous but small number of U.S. personnel to assist the Philippine government in countering the Abu Sayyaf Group (ASG) and other transnational terrorists.

We find that the activities of the U.S. SOF enabled the Philippine government to substantially reduce the transnational terrorist threat in the southern Philippines. U.S. SOF did so by directly supporting Philippine operations and by building capabilities of both its conventional and SOF. U.S. SOF activities contributed to the capture of terrorist-group leaders, decreased enemy attacks, reduced enemy freedom of movement, and increased popular rejection of these groups. These U.S. SOF efforts did not occur in a vacuum; they were complemented by Philippine military and nonmilitary efforts, as well as other U.S. activities, including development and conflict-reduction programs by the U.S. Agency for International Development (USAID) and U.S. military exercises and other security cooperation activities.

## Research Approach

This report documents the activities and operational approaches used by U.S. SOF in OEF-P; it also evaluates their contributions to the outcomes achieved. We employed historical research methods to construct this account, including in-depth interviews with principal U.S. and Philippine actors and extensive exploitation of documents archived at the relevant U.S. command headquarters (HQ).

To measure outcomes, we developed an evaluative framework to assess the activities' effect on (1) the transnational terrorist threat and (2) the PSF's capabilities at the tactical, operational, and institutional levels. For the first outcome, we assessed the counterterrorism (CT) operations' effects on the transnational terrorist groups and on the degree of popular support for the principal threat group and the government forces. The second outcome assesses the development of the PSF's capabilities at the tactical, operational, and institutional levels.

Most official U.S. documents regarding OEF-P remain unavailable to the public, including formal assessments by various U.S. commands, as well as heat maps showing the decreasing areas of freedom of movement of armed groups. However, in this report, we include three types of data to support the findings that U.S. SOF helped to degrade the transnational threat and improve PSF capability. This evidence includes (1) a reduction in adversary attacks, (2) decreased size of the threat group, and (3) declining population support of the threat group and increased satisfaction with government forces. Qualitative judgments by both U.S. and Philippine interviewees form the primary basis for the claim that U.S. SOF contributed to the PSF's improved performance and capability.

## The Operation Enduring Freedom—Philippines Mission

The U.S. SOF mission was to support the Philippine armed forces in countering the terrorist threat in the southern Philippines, which had been plagued by increasing transnational terrorist violence since the mid-1990s. In particular, the ASG had engaged in bombings, extortion, and kidnappings, including of Americans. U.S. forces deployed to the Philippines in February 2002 after extensive negotiations with the Philippine government. Under the terms agreed, military personnel assigned to the U.S. special operations task force (SOTF) were barred from engaging in combat, although they bore arms and retained the right of self-defense. They engaged in three broad categories of activity in what U.S. military doctrine calls *foreign internal defense*:[1] (1) They provided operational advice and direct support to PSF operations against the designated threat groups; (2) they helped train, equip, and improve the Philippine forces' capabilities; and (3) they conducted extensive civil–military operations (CMO) and information operations (IO) in conjunction with Philippine forces to enable combat operations, increase the population's support for the Philippine government, and reduce the safe havens available to the armed groups. In the latter years, the task force (TF) increased its activities to support the institutional development of the PSF in support of the Philippine government's national plan.

---

[1] Joint Publication 1-02 (U.S. Joint Chiefs of Staff, 2015) defines *foreign internal defense* as

> [p]articipation by civilian and military agencies of a government in any of the action programs taken by another government or other designated organization to free and protect its society from subversion, lawlessness, insurgency, terrorism, and other threats to its security.

These multifaceted and geographically dispersed activities included

- operational planning and advice at the three-star joint HQ, as well as at the division, brigade (BDE), and battalion (BN) (and, at times, company) levels, including the creation of fusion cells and other mechanisms to increase the Government of the Republic of the Philippines's (GRP's) joint and interagency coordination
- CMO, including assessments; community outreach; dental, medical, and veterinary care; water, school, and health projects; and construction of roads, bridges, piers, and airstrips
- IO
- intelligence support operations, including intelligence fusion, analysis, and collection via aerial, sea, and ground manned and unmanned intelligence, surveillance, and reconnaissance (ISR) platforms and systems; and maps and secure communications
- medical evacuation (MEDEVAC), emergency medical care, quick reaction, and combat search and rescue (CSAR) via air and maritime mobility platforms that permitted U.S. and Armed Forces of the Philippines (AFP) units to operate throughout a joint operational area that spanned Mindanao, Basilan, Sulu, and Tawi-Tawi
- training of ground combat units in a wide variety of skills
- training of air crews in night-vision capability, forward air control, close air support, and casualty evacuation (CASEVAC) and MEDEVAC
- training of naval forces in maritime interdiction and other operations
- training of police special action forces (SAF)
- intensive training, equipping, institutional support, and advisory assistance to Philippine special operations units—in particular, the Light Reaction forces[2] and the Joint Special Operations Group (JSOG).

---

[2] The Light Reaction Company expanded into the Light Reaction Battalion and is now the Light Reaction Regiment.

A brief summary of OEF-P and its overall effects follows.

## Overview of Operation Enduring Freedom—Philippines

The longstanding U.S.-Philippine military relationship atrophied in the 1990s following the closure of U.S. military bases in 1992. However, the rising incidence of terrorism in the country prompted U.S. officials to offer to assist in improving the Philippine government's CT capability to address a rising threat. Hostage-taking and attacks by the ASG, founded in 1991, and other al Qaeda (AQ)–linked plots in the Philippines, led the Manila government to accept the U.S. proposed assistance to train and equip a CT unit in 2001 before the 9/11 attacks. After the 9/11 attacks, the Philippine president pledged support to the U.S. government in global CT efforts, and the two governments reached agreement on a package of aid and assistance. Under laboriously negotiated terms, approximately 1,300 U.S. forces deployed to the southern Philippines in 2002; thereafter, the effort averaged 500 to 600 troops.

The first phase of OEF-P was focused on the island of Basilan, where the ASG was holding U.S. citizens hostage. Joint Task Force (JTF) 510 deployed for six months to train and advise Philippine forces as they pursued the ASG. In addition to training and advising 15 Philippine Army and Marine Corps battalions that were deployed to Basilan, U.S. SOF, in conjunction with a naval construction task group, carried out extensive CMO all over the island. During this period, U.S. SOF continued to assess PSF capabilities, as well as the threat environment and population of the southern Philippines.

Despite some operational successes on Basilan, the U.S. forces judged that further training, advice, and assistance would be required for the Philippine forces to address the threat. ASG leadership fled to other locations, but the U.S. forces were not permitted to move in pursuit. During 2003–2004, as negotiations for further operational assistance continued, U.S. SOF provided intensive assistance to Philippine SOF—in particular, to build additional companies to form the Light Reaction Battalion. The U.S. SOF also maintained a small, distributed footprint in the southern Philippines in the form of operations and intelligence fusion teams (OIFTs) located at various command HQ.

In 2005, JSOTF-Philippines (JSOTF-P) moved south to Camp General Basilio Navarro in Zamboanga, the capital of Mindanao, which would serve as the hub of the effort for the remaining years of OEF-P. Pursuant to an assessment conducted by its higher HQ, Special Operations Command, Pacific (SOCPAC), JSOTF-P began to apply the same population-centric approach it used in Basilan to Jolo, the main island of the Sulu archipelago, where ASG activities were most intense. In addition, U.S. SOF expanded advisory activities in central Mindanao. Additional activities included maritime interdiction operations and training, advising, and equipping of naval special operations units. Between 2005 and 2007, the PSF, supported by JSOTF-P, achieved notable successes on Jolo in removing key ASG leadership and reducing the group's freedom of movement. In a major change of approach, the AFP shifted the balance of their efforts from largely kinetic combat operations to an approach that favored CMO, such as the U.S. SOF had employed. The AFP also developed training courses and doctrine for CMO.

Although AFP capabilities were judged to be improving, Philippine forces still lacked the ability to find, fix, and finish terrorist targets with a minimum of collateral damage. From 2008 to 2010, JSOTF-P focused on a variety of programs to remedy those deficits. This included an increase in U.S. intelligence support, a program to provide a precision-strike capability, and an array of advisory efforts to the Philippine Air Force (PAF) to enhance air–ground coordination. CMO and IO continued in a decentralized manner and greater focus was placed on central Mindanao, where hostilities had flared. There, as on Basilan and Jolo, the ASG and Jemaah Islamiyah (JI) had found sanctuary, support, and recruits among the separatist armed groups that had rejected the government's peace overtures.

In 2011, the U.S. and Phillippine governments decided that the primary objectives of the SOF mission had been met. In response, JSOTF-P began several new initiatives to nest its plans and activities under the U.S. embassy civilian efforts, as well as those of the Philippine government. A new training and advisory effort focused on building special police forces and creating fusion cells to increase cooperation between police and military forces. The overall JSOTF-P advisory effort drew back from tactical echelons to focus on operational HQ and institutional development.

In 2013, an attack by a rogue element of the Moro National Liberation Front (MNLF) and a major typhoon slowed transition efforts. The Philippine government's handling of the uprising and hostage crisis demonstrated its forces' ability to plan and conduct operations jointly and with the police. The typhoon underscored the utility of a forward SOF presence with the understanding, mobility, communications, and other assets that could be pressed into service for humanitarian and disaster relief. Transition preparation resumed, although the U.S. embassy expressed concern about its ability to implement programs in the south and ensure mobility and force protection for its personnel after the withdrawal of JSOTF-P.

Some Philippine and U.S. officials also expressed concern that the withdrawal could lead to a resurgence of a renewed terrorist threat, possibly sparked by aggressive propaganda and recruitment by the Islamic State of Iraq and the Levant (ISIL). To mitigate these risks, JSOTF-P proposed a variety of measures to maintain situational awareness and continue supporting the PSF following the deactivation of the TF. A gradual transition was implemented in 2013 and 2014 whereby the number of JSOTF-P personnel was decreased, outstations closed, and warm bases maintained for expeditionary SOF presence. The U.S. Pacific Command Augmentation Team (PAT), based at the U.S. embassy in Manila, assumed responsibility for the remaining personnel and activities after the deactivation of JSOTF-P in February 2015.

## Findings

We find that the U.S. SOF activities in the Philippines between 2001 and 2014 contributed to (1) a reduced transnational terrorist threat and support for threat groups and (2) increased PSF capabilities at the tactical, operational, and institutional levels. The continuous presence and activities of JSOTF-P correlates with the changes in the threat level and threat conditions during the period studied, compared with a rising threat level in the mid- to late 1990s. Independent polls also indicated that the population overwhelmingly and increasingly rejected the terrorist group and supported the government. The increased Philippine capability is demonstrated by multiple successful operations and increased joint planning and assessment capability; U.S. and Philippine interviewees judged that U.S. SOF contributed directly to increased Philippine security capabilities in a variety of ways.

### Reduced Transnational Threat and Threat Conditions

The primary evidence that we cite to support these findings is (1) a reduction in enemy-initiated attacks, (2) decreased numbers of ASG militants, and (3) polls showing reduced support for the ASG and a substantial majority reporting satisfaction with the PSF:

- According to data collected by the Empirical Studies of Conflict (ESOC) project for the Philippines, enemy-initiated attacks in the ASG's three primary areas of operation (Basilan, Sulu, and Tawi-Tawi) declined 56 percent between 2000 and 2012 (see Figure S.1) (ESOC, undated). The attack-rate decline was not linear, and southern Basilan continues to be an area of unrest.
- The number of ASG-armed militants declined from an estimated 1,270 to 437 members, according to the AFP. The U.S. State Department annual reports estimate that the ASG declined from more than 2,200 to 400 armed members (Headquarters, WestMinCom, undated).[3]
- Independent polls show increased support for the PSF and decreased support for the ASG by a large majority of the population in areas where the ASG was most active. In 2011, U.S. SOF contracted an independent polling firm to assess public opinion in six "conflict-affected areas" of the Mindanao region; this

[3] Other sources cite lower numbers of ASG militants as of 2014. For example, "Country Reports on Terrorism 2013" (U.S. Department of State, 2014) estimated the number of ASG members at 400. Its 2000 report, *Patterns of Global Terrorism*, estimated the number at "more than 2,000" (U.S. Department of State, 2001). The Associated Press put the number of ASG even lower, at 300 (Gomez, 2014).

**Figure S.1**
**Enemy-Initiated Attacks in Basilan, Sulu, and Tawi-Tawi, 2000–2012**

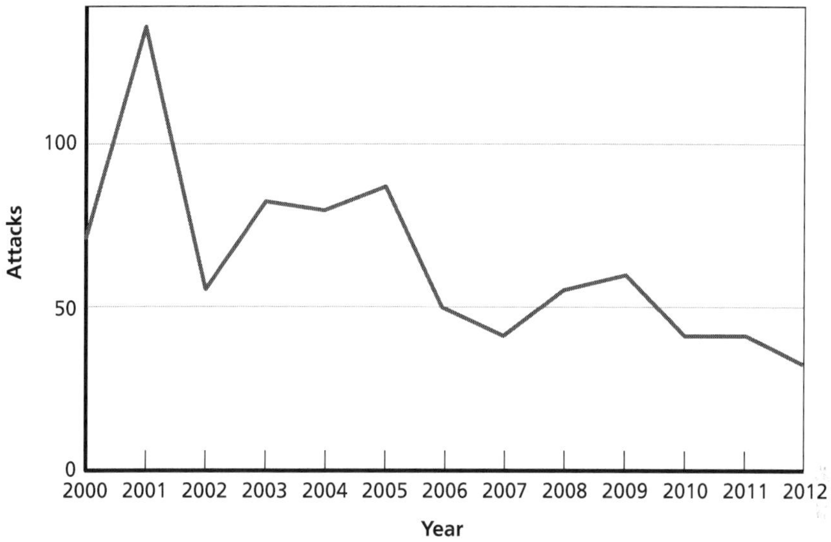


SOURCE: ESOC data.
NOTE: Attack data are for all threat groups in Basilian, Sulu, and Tawi-Tawi provinces between 2000 and 2012. The total number of attacks in these three provinces declined from 73 in 2000 to 32 in 2012. Data are not available for 2013 or 2014. Subsequent chapters include data by time period, and Chapter Eight shows the trends by province.
RAND *RR1236-S.1*

Southern Philippines Public Perception Survey found that the number of those who reported being satisfied with the Philippine security services increased from 51 percent in 2011 to 63 percent in 2014. In the same time period, the number of those expressing trust in the ASG declined from 8 percent to 2.5 percent (Teutsch and Thambidurai, 2014, pp. 59, 74).[4] Focus groups suggested that improved security forces, medical care, and infrastructure were among the benefits provided by the U.S. SOF presence.

---

[4] In addition, 86 percent of respondents said that the AFP were making their area safer, and 79 percent said the Philippine National Police (PNP) were making their area safer (pp. 42, 36).

Numerous interviewees cited heat maps constructed with data collected and compiled by JSOTF-P that indicated reduced freedom of movement for the ASG throughout the southern Philippines. This reduced freedom of movement correlates with the areas of intensive CMO by both U.S. and Philippine forces.

Finally, a qualitative assessment shared by both U.S. and Philippine commanders viewed the ASG as having evolved from a transnational threat to a largely criminal organization that conducts illegal activities primarily to sustain itself.

Progress in reducing the transnational terrorist threat and improving the PSF was neither linear nor complete. Over the course of the 14-year effort, the so-called balloon effect could be observed as the locus of the threat, and high-value individuals moved from one island to another. Over time, consistent application of sound counterinsurgency practices that denied the enemy the support of the population (and rival armed groups), resources, and sanctuaries gradually increased the effectiveness of AFP operations and shrank the threat groups' room for maneuver. However, both Philippine and U.S. officers interviewed believed that a resurgent terrorist threat was possible under certain conditions and that continued vigilance and application of sound counterinsurgency practices were warranted.

**Increased Philippine Security Force Capabilities**

From 2001 to 2014, the PSF increased their capabilities at the tactical, operational, and institutional levels, albeit to differing degrees. U.S. SOF contributed to this increased capability by providing training, advice, assistance, and some equipment. The primary evidence supporting this finding is assessments by U.S. and Philippine military officers who were interviewed, supported by official documentation, as well as operational results.

At the tactical level, U.S. SOF provided training, advice, and assistance to conventional AFP units at all echelons throughout Mindanao, including Philippine Army, Philippine Marine Corps, Philippine Navy, and PAF units. In the later years of OEF-P, U.S. SOF also provided training, advice, and assistance to the PNP SAF. The most-intensive tactical training, advice, and assistance, as well as equipment, were provided to the various elements of the Philippine SOF, particularly the Light Reaction Regiment (LRR) and, to a lesser degree, the naval special operations group (SOG), the First Scout Ranger Regiment (1st SRR), and the Special Forces Regiment (SFR). The Philippine special operations units were considered the most tactically proficient elements of the AFP.[5] U.S. SOF interviewees judged that Philippine SOF are among the most proficient of those Asian SOF units with which they had worked.

At the operational level, U.S. SOF advised and assisted the AFP HQ to improve its joint processes and integrate command and control (C2), planning, and intelligence functions. U.S. SOF assisted and provided equipment for the Western Mindanao Command (WestMinCom) to establish a joint operations center and lower-echelon fusion centers that included police, as well as to integrate air–ground operations. The advisory functions extended to WestMinCom's lower echelons, including JTF Comet and division and brigade staffs. U.S. SOF also provided intensive advice and assistance in the creation of the JSOG and operational HQ.

At the institutional level, U.S. SOF contributed somewhat to strategy, planning, and coordination at the AFP national HQ, and they helped WestMinCom develop its plans and intelligence analysis and fusion capabilities. U.S. SOF assisted most intensively in the institutional development of Philippine SOF force-providing HQ, including Special Operations Command Philippine Army (SOCOM PA); and the Philippine Army SOF HQ; as well as the institutions and processes to create a self-sustaining SOF enterprise. With U.S. SOF assistance, Philippine SOF developed a training cadre, schoolhouse, selection criteria, courses, doctrine, and a noncommissioned-officer (NCO) academy. U.S. SOF also assisted in the later years in the creation of the AFP's CMO capability, including courses, doctrine, and development of subject-matter expertise.

Although it is possible that the PSF could have developed these capabilities without U.S. SOF's assistance, current and former AFP

---

[5] One empirical analysis found that Philippine SOF achieved higher enemy casualty rates with lower civilian and friendly casualties. See Felter, 2009.

officers who served at various echelons of conventional and special operations units stated that their command staffs and leaders gained increased proficiency in fusing intelligence and operations and planning and executing complex operations with the assistance of U.S. SOF. They stated that the training, advice, intelligence, and equipment that U.S. SOF provided to the PSF had increased their capabilities and troops' confidence and lowered casualty and mortality rates.

A significant gap remains in joint operations and even more so in police–military coordination, as well as the overall proficiency and reputation of PNP, which consistently ranks lower than the military in opinion polls conducted by the U.S. State Department. U.S.-instituted fusion cells enhanced cooperation with the police in Mindanao but, according to both U.S. and Philippine interviewees and the evidence of several operations, including the high-casualty January 2015 operation, military–police cooperation and coordination remained insufficient.[6] Furthermore, both U.S. and Philippine interviewees doubted that PNP would be ready to assume responsibility nationwide for internal security by 2016, as called for in the Philippine *Internal Peace and Security Plan* (IPSP) (AFP, 2010).

### Enhanced Bilateral Defense Ties

In addition to reducing the terrorist threat and producing more-capable PSF, the U.S. SOF effort likely contributed to a third outcome of strengthened U.S.-Philippine military relations. Virtually every senior Philippine military officer served at least one combat tour in the southern Philippines between 2002 and 2014 and continued to have contact with U.S. SOF as they progressed upward in their careers. U.S. military and civilian officials noted that the experience of continuous U.S. assistance under OEF-P also likely diminished the Filipinos' previous concerns regarding the U.S. military presence in the Philippines, which had led to the base closures in 1991. Focus groups conducted by

---

[6] During an ill-fated operation on January 24, 2015, 44 PNP SAF troops were ambushed and killed after a successful operation that killed the top JI target in the country, a Malaysian facilitator known as Marwan, whose real name was Zulkifli bin Hir. The deaths and ensuing national debate dimmed prospects for ratification of the terms of a peace agreement concluded with the Moro Islamic Liberation Front (MILF) in 2014.

an independent polling firm in 2014 found that residents in Mindanao would welcome an increased presence, largely based on their views of the security, infrastructure, medical, and other benefits of the U.S. SOF activities there (TNS Qualitative, 2014, p. 32). Other factors, such as rising concern in the Philippines about China's activities in the South China Sea, were also cited as contributing to the closer U.S.-Philippine bilateral relationship and defense ties in particular. In 2014, the two governments signed the Enhanced Defense Cooperation agreement (GRP and United States, 2014) that provided for increased U.S. exercises, troop presence, and security cooperation in the Philippines.

### Other U.S. Government and Philippine Contributions

The findings that U.S. SOF contributed to these positive outcomes do not exclude the contributing effects of other U.S. or Philippine government inputs. U.S. SOF activities were not solely responsible for the improved security picture or the improved security capabilities. The Philippine government took steps unilaterally that contributed to the effectiveness of PSF—notably, to increase material support to PSF and promulgate a national plan that sought to implement a whole-of-society approach to resolving conflict in the south. The government improved its standing among the population more generally as it implanted reforms and greater consideration of human rights after a history of military rule and coup attempts. However, ongoing problems exist, including corruption and a legacy of mistrust and neglect.

In addition, the U.S. government's nonmilitary contributions were substantial. USAID provided most U.S. assistance, and the majority of its aid in this period was directed to the southern Philippines. The largest program, Growth with Equity in Mindanao (GEM), totaled $180.9 million between 2002 and 2012. A follow-on grant of $127.7 million began in 2012 to support the Mindanao Peace and Development Program. Specific projects included medium- and small-scale infrastructure, workforce preparation, businesses (such as aquaculture), and governance improvement. The Arms to Farms program supported training for former MNLF combatants. The U.S. Departments of State and Justice undertook police training programs. The U.S. embassy also coordinated its military and nonmilitary programs and activities through the Mindanao Working Group, led by the deputy chief of mission.

**Key Limiting and Contributing Factors**

We identified three factors that limited the positive outcomes to which OEF-P contributed. First, OEF-P focused substantial efforts on institutionalizing of PSF capabilities only in the later years. An earlier emphasis on staff and institutional development, as opposed to tactical capabilities, might have hastened PSF development and permitted an earlier transition. Gaps remain in PSF coordination of joint, police, and special operations forces. A second and related limiting factor is that the security-force assistance efforts that JSOTF-P undertook were not closely aligned with U.S. embassy security assistance efforts or AFP decisions on military hardware purchases. Third, U.S. efforts could not overcome the fact that underlying drivers of conflict, such as crime, poverty, discrimination, and other grievances, continue to exist despite the Philippine government's efforts to address them.

We identified four factors that contributed significantly to the outcomes that OEF-P did achieve in combination with Philippine and other U.S. government actions. OEF-P observed a cardinal principle of foreign internal defense from inception; the mission was conducted in support of the Philippine government and through the PSF. This respect for Philippine sovereignty was enshrined in the terms of reference, without which the mission would not have begun or continued. This key factor informed the rules of engagement (ROE), which permitted battalion- and, at times, company-level advising and direct support on the battlefield but not combat by U.S. forces (who did retain the right of self-defense). We conclude that these ROE were adequate to permit robust support to the partner while avoiding the dependency that might have resulted from U.S. troops in a direct combat advisory role (assuming that the political environment had permitted it). Finally, this principle of respect for the sovereign lead also dictated support for Philippine government policies of negotiating with the Moro separatist groups MNLF and MILF, even though this created a complex environment for U.S. SOF to navigate, particularly when those groups provided tacit or overt support to transnational terrorist groups that were the object of OEF-P.

A second key contributing factor was the consistent emphasis that U.S. SOF placed on conducting rigorous and regular assessments to inform their campaign design and subsequent adaptations to the plan. This commitment to operational design at all echelons allowed for both continuity of effort in the broad objectives and adaptation as warranted by the changing situation and impact of operations.

Third, U.S. SOF applied a holistic approach rather than a narrow counterterrorism approach to the mission, which included training, advice and assistance to all relevant services and units, as well as robust civil military and information operations.

Fourth, JSOTF-P and the U.S. country team made concerted efforts to work together and create mechanisms for collaboration and deconfliction. Efforts taken by JSOTF-P included regular visits to Manila, placement of staff liaisons at the embassy, participation in country team–led working groups, and hosting of country-team members at JSOTF-P HQ in Mindanao. In addition, as ambassadors and other members of the country team acknowledged, JSOTF-P directly supported U.S. country-team programs by providing force protection, mobility, and monitoring of projects that U.S. civilian officials would have been otherwise unable to visit. Most of the U.S. military and civilian interviewees considered that the efforts made to create a synergistic interagency effort by both U.S. SOF and members of the country team exceeded those efforts made elsewhere, in their experiences.[7] However, interviewees also cited frictions that occurred at times over such issues as failure to tap the embassy's expertise; confer on country need assessments; agree on development priorities; and observe embassy guidance on public affairs, public diplomacy, or protocol matters.

---

[7] An independent evaluation commissioned by USAID stated, "USAID and the Joint Special Operations Task Force—Philippines work closely together in several conflict areas of Mindanao to support the Philippine development objectives." See USAID, undated, pp. 4–5.

## Generalizability of Findings

Although the scope of this study did not include testing the generalizability of these findings, they might apply to some degree to some other cases of long-duration special operations in countries that possess some capability and political will to lead security operations.[8] The feasibility, scale, and duration of foreign internal defense depend heavily on not only the will and nature of its government but also the capability, nature, and will of the forces being supported. Recent efforts in Colombia, Yemen, east and west Africa, and the Middle East offer points of comparison and contrast. The Philippines and Colombia represent cases in which relatively intact governments found the will and resources to lead such efforts, despite facing severe security, corruption, and long-running socioeconomic challenges.

The Philippines has a history of military rule, a more-recent incidence of coup attempts, some degree of anti-Americanism, a widely reported phenomenon of official corruption among civilian and military institutions, and a history of ethnosectarian conflict in the south. Nonetheless, these negative factors were not severe enough to impede the outcomes achieved by sustained and multifaceted advisory and operational assistance and CMO of JSOTF-P in support of AFP operations in the south and the development of one of Asia's most-competent joint SOF (interview 42, September 30, 2014; interview 41, October 11, 2014).[9] The experience of U.S. SOF in the Philippines represents a positive return on a relatively small investment, as well as a possible model that might apply, with appropriate adjustments, to similarly motivated and relatively capable countries that seek assistance to address transnational or internal security threats.

Granting that the host government will likely need to meet certain bars for the successful application of foreign internal defense, the features that might be most fungible are the U.S. forces' consistent

---

[8] One comparative study suggests that there are significant limits to generalizability. See Watts et al., 2014.

[9] These interviewees, who participated in training and advising of a half-dozen special operations units in Asia over the past 20 years, rated the Philippine forces just after Singapore's forces in overall competence.

application of principles of operational design and the synergistic application of varied special operations capabilities and other enablers.

In this regard, OEF-P can be considered a textbook example of *how* to conduct foreign internal defense, specifically through the synergistic application of diverse special operations capabilities, as well as appropriate use of assessments.

This case also illustrates the difference between security cooperation and foreign internal defense. Security cooperation is distinguished by activities that build capability and interoperability but do not employ those capabilities. In contrast, foreign internal defense entails an operational focus distinguished primarily by (1) providing operational assistance to forces engaged in combat and (2) conducting CMO and IO. In this case, partner-building train-and-equip activities are harnessed to operational activities and objectives. In OEF-P, a sufficiently robust advisory force was authorized to carry out all of these functions and provide *direct support to the partner's operations* in various locations, to multiple echelons and various security forces, with the goal of enabling the Philippine forces to achieve the government's objectives in a sustainable manner.

In sum, the OEF-P case demonstrates how a small number of U.S. forces employed in this manner can assist another government in achieving effects at multiple echelons, in multiple forces, and over a wide geographic area without assuming a combat role. The report identifies a temporal requirement, as well as a need for periodic adaptation to address a dynamic, persistent, and mobile threat while maintaining overall continuity of effort. Although U.S. SOF provided most of the TF's manpower and conducted the widest array of activities, U.S. conventional forces and contracted services played significant roles. The report identifies the positive outcomes correlated with this effort, in terms of a reduced threat, a more capable security force, and a population that rejects terrorist groups. We also identify contributing factors and limiting factors.

# Acknowledgments

We would like to thank the Office of the Assistant Secretary of Defense for Special Operations/Low-Intensity Conflict and, in particular, its director of special operations and irregular warfare, COL Brad L. Reed, and LTC Varman S. Chhoeung for supporting this study, as well as the commander of Special Operations Command, Pacific, RDML Colin J. Kilrain; deputy commander COL Robert Bond; LTC Peter B. Tingstrom; LTC Bo Gardner; Christine Geilfuss; and all the staff at Special Operations Command, Pacific, who provided interviews and research assistance. We are also grateful to the commander of Joint Special Operations Task Force—Philippines COL Erik M. Brown, operations chief MAJ Judd C. Floris, all the Joint Special Operations Task Force—Philippines personnel who agreed to be interviewed and provided support, and the Center for Army Analysis. In the United States, U.S. Army Special Operations Command commanding general LTG Charles T. Cleveland, U.S. Air Force Special Operations Command commanding general Lt Gen Eric E. Fiel, Naval Special Warfare Command commander RADM Brian L. Losey, and U.S. Army Special Forces Command commanding general BG Darsie D. Rogers permitted interviews with personnel who served previously in Operation Enduring Freedom—Philippines, including 1st Special Forces Group (Airborne), Naval Special Warfare teams, 95th Civil Affairs Brigade (Airborne), Military Information Support Operations Command, U.S. Air Force Special Operations 6th Special Operations Squadron and other U.S. Air Force Special Operations Command personnel. We are particularly indebted to several retired senior officials who generously gave their time and materials from their own archives to support our research: Lt Gen Donald C. Wurster, LTG David P. Fridovich, Ambassador Francis J. Ricciardone, Col David W. Maxwell, COL Joseph H. Felter III, and LTC Dennis Downey. We thank the large number of active-duty military personnel and civilian officials in the U.S. government, as well as the Government of the Republic of the Philippines, for interviews and access to their documents, bases, personnel, and other research support to this project. In accordance with study guidelines, we conducted the interviews with active-duty personnel and serving U.S. officials under nonattribution rules. We are extremely grateful to our peer reviewers, Center for American Progress vice president Vikram J. Singh and RAND senior political scientist Stephen Watts, for their thoughtful critiques and many constructive suggestions, which greatly improved the final product. Finally, we appreciate the research assistance provided by RAND colleagues Jeremy Boback, James Hoobler, and Philip Padilla and thank the leadership of the RAND International Security and Defense Policy Center; the publications department, including Lisa Bernard; and Amanda Hagerman-Thompson for their meticulous efforts on behalf of this study.

## Abbreviations

| | |
|---|---|
| 1st SRR | First Scout Ranger Regiment |
| AFP | Armed Forces of the Philippines |
| AFSOC | U.S. Air Force Special Operations Command |
| AOB | advanced operational base |
| AOR | area of responsibility |
| AQ | al Qaeda |
| ARMM | Autonomous Region in Muslim Mindanao |
| ARSOF | U.S. Army special operations forces |
| ASG | Abu Sayyaf Group |
| BDE | brigade |
| BIFF | Bangsamoro Islamic Freedom Fighters |
| BN | battalion |
| C2 | command and control |
| CA | civil affairs |
| CAB | Comprehensive Agreement on the Bangsamoro |
| CASEVAC | casualty evacuation |
| CMO | civil–military operations |

| | |
|---|---|
| CSAR | combat search and rescue |
| CT | counterterrorism |
| Det | detachment |
| DoD | U.S. Department of Defense |
| EastMinCom | Eastern Mindanao Command |
| ESOC | Empirical Studies of Conflict |
| FWD | forward |
| FY | fiscal year |
| GEM | Growth with Equity in Mindanao |
| GHQ | general headquarters |
| GRP | Government of the Republic of the Philippines |
| HQ | headquarters |
| HSP | Human Subject Protections |
| HUMINT | human intelligence |
| IMINT | imagery intelligence |
| IO | information operations |
| IPSP | Internal Peace and Security Plan |
| ISIL | Islamic State of Iraq and the Levant |
| ISR | intelligence, surveillance, and reconnaissance |
| J-2 | intelligence directorate |
| J-3 | operations directorate |
| JCET | joint combined exchange training |
| JI | Jemaah Islamiyah |
| JITF-M | Joint Intelligence Task Force—Mindanao |

| | |
|---|---|
| JOA | joint operations area |
| JSOAD | Joint Special Operations Air Detachment |
| JSOG | Joint Special Operations Group |
| JSOTF | joint special operations task force |
| JSOTF-P | Joint Special Operations Task Force—Philippines |
| JTF | joint task force |
| JUSMAG | joint U.S. military assistance group |
| LCE | liaison coordination element |
| LEGAT | legal attaché |
| LNO | liaison officer |
| LRC | light reaction company |
| LRR | Light Reaction Regiment |
| MEDCAP | medical civic action program |
| MEDEVAC | medical evacuation |
| MILF | Moro Islamic Liberation Front |
| MISO | military information support operations |
| MIST | military information support team |
| MNLF | Moro National Liberation Front |
| MSOT | U.S. Marine Corps special operations team |
| NAVSOG | Naval Special Operations Group |
| NCO | noncommissioned officer |
| NCTG | naval construction task group |
| NDAA | National Defense Authorization Act |

| | |
|---|---|
| NPA | New People's Army |
| NSW | naval special warfare |
| NVG | night-vision goggles |
| ODA | operational detachment—alpha |
| OEF-P | Operation Enduring Freedom—Philippines |
| OIFT | operations and intelligence fusion team |
| PA | Philippine Army |
| PAF | Philippine Air Force |
| PAT | U.S. Pacific Command Augmentation Team |
| PE | preparation of the environment |
| PLT | platoon |
| PNP | Philippine National Police |
| PSF | Philippine Security Forces |
| PSYOP | psychological operations |
| QRF | quick-reaction force |
| RIB | rubberized inflatable boat |
| ROE | rules of engagement |
| SAF | special action force |
| SDO | senior defense officer |
| SEAL | sea, air, and land |
| SF | special forces |
| SFG | Special Forces Group |
| SFR | Special Forces Regiment |
| SIGINT | signals intelligence |

| | |
|---|---|
| SOCOM | Special Operations Command |
| SOCPAC | Special Operations Command, Pacific |
| SOF | special operations forces |
| SOG | special operations group |
| SOTF | special operations task force |
| SOUTHCOM | U.S. Southern Command |
| SRR | scout ranger regiment |
| TCAV | terrorism coordination and assistance visit |
| TDY | temporary duty |
| TF | task force |
| TG | task group |
| UAV | unmanned aerial vehicle |
| USAID | U.S. Agency for International Development |
| USCINCPAC | commander in chief of U.S. Pacific Command |
| USPACOM | U.S. Pacific Command |
| VETCAP | veterinary civic action program |
| VFA | visiting-forces agreement |
| WestMinCom | Western Mindanao Command |

CHAPTER ONE

# Introduction

## Study Purpose

This study examined the 14-year experience of U.S. special operations forces (SOF) in the Philippines from 2001 through 2014. The objective of this case history is to document and evaluate the activities and effects of special operations capabilities employed to address terrorist threats in Operation Enduring Freedom—Philippines (OEF-P) through (1) training and equipping Philippine Security Forces (PSF), (2) providing operational advice and enablers, and (3) conducting civil–military operations (CMO) and information operations (IO). The purpose of this case history, in addition to providing an authoritative and comprehensive record of a long-duration special operations mission, is to inform future U.S. government policymaking and military planning regarding the employment of SOF to counter terrorist threats in partnership with another government. This report is also designed for use in professional military education, particularly for commanders and planners who might be charged with similar efforts in the future.[1]

Small numbers of U.S. SOF deployed continuously during OEF-P. Their mission was to counter transnational threats in the southern Philippines through support to the Philippine government and armed forces.

The mission entailed working alongside PSF in a variety of ways to counter terrorist threats—in particular, those posed by the Abu

[1] This report follows a similar format to that of a previous RAND report that is not available to the public.

Sayyaf Group (ASG) and elements of Jemaah Islamiyah (JI) that supported their activities. In this case, U.S. forces were not permitted to engage in combat, but they were authorized to support Philippine operations and engage with the population. This application of U.S. force is described in U.S. military doctrine as *foreign internal defense*, in which U.S. objectives are achieved by activities conducted in support of a partner- or host-nation force (U.S. Joint Chiefs of Staff, 2010). Under this doctrine, U.S. SOF aimed to directly and indirectly affect the threat by contributing to the partner actions and capabilities. Three specific types of activities were undertaken throughout OEF-P: (1) U.S. CMO and IO were conducted to increase government access and reduce adversary access to and support from the population, territory, and resources; (2) U.S. SOF enabled Philippine security operations by providing advice, intelligence, mobility platforms, communications, and medical care; and (3) U.S. SOF helped build capability through training and equipping Philippine conventional, special, and police forces.

## Research Approach

The Office of the Assistant Secretary of Defense for Special Operations/Low-Intensity Conflict asked us to document one of the longest-duration special operations missions and evaluate its impact. We framed three research questions: What did U.S. SOF do in the Philippines between 2001 and 2014? How did they conduct their mission (i.e., what approaches did they apply in these activities)? And what impact did they have? We used historical research methods to construct a comprehensive, authoritative account relying principally on firsthand sources and documents, including in-depth interviews with participants and official documents. We also consulted multiple additional sources, including published documents and academic literature, to verify key points and compensate for the inherent bias of participant interviews.

To produce a comprehensive and authoritative account, we were granted wide access to interview subjects and documentation in the

United States and in the Philippines. We conducted interviews in the United States and the Philippines from October 2014 to January 2015 and collected and analyzed official documents at several command headquarters (HQ) to construct a detailed historical narrative that identified the principal activities of U.S. SOF and other U.S. government entities; the Philippine government and its forces; and the adversaries, with particular focus on the transnational threat groups. We conducted in-depth individual and group interviews with approximately 150 key U.S. and Philippine participants in OEF-P from 2001 through 2014. These included commanders, staff officers, and noncommissioned officers (NCOs) at all echelons; U.S. ambassadors and other civilian officials; and senior Philippine officials, senior and junior officers, and civilians. We included in the sample special operations personnel from all services with experience in all geographic locations of OEF-P activities. All special operations functional specialties were represented.

In order to document special operations activities in detail, we conducted the majority of interviews with U.S. military personnel assigned to special operations units; another 25 percent of interviewees were other Americans or Filipinos, including civilians and civilian officials. Human Subject Protections (HSP) protocols have been used in this report in accordance with the appropriate statutes and DOD regulations governing HSP. Therefore, interviewees are identified as SOF or non-SOF and U.S. or Philippine. These sources' views are solely their own and do not represent the official policy or position of DOD, the U.S. Government or any foreign government.

The interviews and a rich array of documents enabled us to develop a detailed account of both what SOF did and how they did it. We examined the approaches that SOF used, including application of SOF doctrine on foreign internal defense, as well as the principles of operational design, which relies on assessments as a tool for problem framing, plan formulation, and plan adaptation. We designed the interview protocol to enable us to identify not only plans, operations, and activities but also the evolution in the approach that U.S. SOF employed during those 14 years, the reasons for those changes, and the apparent results achieved.

We therefore asked SOF interviewees to describe any mission analysis or other preparatory activities they undertook; their role in plan development (if any); their role in plan execution, i.e., operations and activities; whether any assessment was conducted and, if so, what adaptations were made pursuant to that assessment; and, finally, what, if any, outcomes or results were observed regarding the threat, the partner capacity and capability, and the overall partner relationship. We asked the interviewees to describe any unsuccessful initiatives or results contrary to the objectives and any explanation for those outcomes, if known. In addition, we asked interviewees whether U.S. and partner objectives diverged and, if so, how this divergence was handled.

We asked non-SOF interviewees to provide detailed accounts of U.S. government and Philippine plans, activities, assessments, and coordination with U.S. SOF; how they viewed SOF efforts in the context of larger U.S. and Philippine objectives; what, if any, impact SOF activities had on their own activities and efforts; and what impact, if any, U.S. SOF activities had on the threat, partner capability, and the bilateral relationship. We asked the non-SOF interviewees whether their plans and activities evolved over time, whether U.S. SOF activities evolved, and whether U.S. SOF activities contributed to U.S. government and Philippine government objectives. We also asked them whether U.S. and Philippine objectives diverged and, if so, how any divergence was handled. Finally, we asked interviewees to describe any unsuccessful initiatives and provide an explanation, if known, for the lack of success. Philippine interviewees also provided perspectives on national plans, actions, and results, as well as background information on the region, groups, and conflict history. Many interviewees provided perspectives on different time periods within the 14-year effort, including comparative observations; most of the SOF personnel served more than one tour and, in many cases, up to four tours. Many U.S. embassy personnel, including the four U.S. ambassadors, served multiyear tours between 2002 and 2014. Most of the Philippine officials interviewed had served in multiple relevant positions in Mindanao, Manila, and other locations during the time period studied.

We extensively exploited several hundred documents to evaluate and provide further context for the interview data. We collected documents from several command HQ, including Joint Special Operations Task Force—Philippines (JSOTF-P); Special Operations Command, Pacific (SOCPAC); U.S. Pacific Command (USPACOM); and Western Mindanao Command (WestMinCom). We compared the interview results with information in hundreds of documents collected from the U.S. commands, including command plans, assessments, briefings, end-of-tour reports, a 500-page chronology, surveys, and other material spanning the 14-year time period. In addition, we consulted academic research and other published literature, including Philippine academic research and literature.

We developed the following framework to evaluate the effects of the U.S. special operations activities. The mission aimed to improve and support PSF's ability to counter transnational terrorist groups in the southern Philippines, so the evaluative framework assesses both counterterrorism (CT) and capacity-building outcomes. We assessed the trajectory of CT operations, the effects on the transnational terrorist groups, and the population's support for them. We also assessed the development of PSF's capabilities at the tactical, operational, and institutional levels.

We cite data to support the findings. Many U.S. documents are not available to the public, including formal assessments by various U.S. commands, as well as heat maps showing the decreasing areas of freedom of movement of armed groups. However, three types of data support the findings of a degraded transnational terrorist threat and an improved PSF capability: (1) a reduction in enemy attacks, (2) decreased size of the threat group, and (3) declining population support of the threat group and increased satisfaction with government forces.

The development of security force capability relies primarily on the qualitative judgments of participant interviewees; these judgments, as well as successful operational outcomes, constitute the primary evidence that PSF increased their capabilities at the tactical, operational, and institutional levels and that U.S. SOF contributed significantly to those increased capabilities and operational effectiveness. No assertion rests on a single interview source, and we base the major findings not only on SOF judgments but also other U.S. and Philippine judgments, including published sources. In some cases, only personnel assigned to the U.S. special operations task force (SOTF) possessed knowledge of specific activities undertaken by the task force (TF); in all of these cases, documentation collected from the commands (for example, regarding the utility of a specific intelligence asset) support the assertions that SOF personnel made in interviews. We adopted these standards to minimize distortions based on the inherent bias of individual interviews. We note conflicting views.

## Organization of the Report

We have organized the account chronologically. Each chapter examines the approach applied by U.S. SOF during that time period, including its assessment, planning and plan adaptation, and plan execution. Each chapter concludes with a summary of results achieved at that time in that location or functional area. The final chapter provides a summary of the outcomes achieved over the 14 years, the supporting evidence, and the key enabling and limiting factors.

Chapter Two provides an overview of the historical conditions, the bilateral relationship, and the relevant U.S. decisions and military activities that set the stage for Operation Enduring Freedom. Chapter Three introduces the preliminary inputs provided by the various partners, the initial assessment conducted by U.S. forces, the launch of OEF-P under Joint TF (JTF) 5-10 and the follow-on efforts taken in 2003 and 2004. Chapter Four identifies the primary inputs of 2005 to 2007, including the 2005 assessment and move to Jolo, the conduct of Operation Ultimatum, and the results achieved there and on Basilan. Chapter Five identifies the primary inputs of 2008 to 2010, starting with the USPACOM assessment of 2008, further expansion of geographically distributed operations, the drive to supply PSF with new precision-strike capabilities, and results achieved or correlated with these efforts.

Chapter Six identifies primary inputs for the period 2010 to 2012, including a concerted effort to mesh Philippine, U.S. embassy, and special operations plans and activities as a necessary precursor to transition. This entailed a new effort to create police special action forces (SAF), initiation of institutional-level advising, intensified embassy coordination, and the fruition of the close air support precision-guided munition capability. Chapter Seven identifies the primary transition activities in 2012 to 2014 that became the focus of the SOTF, including closure of outstations, reduction of personnel, and transfer of responsibilities to other U.S. and Philippine entities. At that time, the TF returned to an expeditionary model for supplying operational advisory assistance out of cold and warm bases. The Zamboanga siege in 2013 tested the Philippine ability to marshal a joint military and police response, and Typhoon Yolanda shortly thereafter illustrated the utility of a special operations presence to provide early assessments, lift, and other assistance in a disaster-relief operation. Final assessments and decisions paved the way for the end of JSOTF-P, which was replaced by a robust USPACOM Augmentation Team (PAT) with an intelligence support team in the southern Philippines to provide early warning of potential resurgent threats.

Chapter Eight concludes the study with an overview of the principal U.S. inputs and best practices developed over 14 years, the principal outcomes, and the deficits in the U.S. and Philippine approaches. Appendix A reproduces excerpts of the Balikatan terms of reference, and a study guide included in Appendix B poses questions for use in planning and professional military education to facilitate analysis of the strengths and weakness of the plan design, execution, assessment, and adaptation.

CHAPTER TWO

# U.S.-Philippine Relations in Historical Perspective

The United States and the Philippines have maintained a close but complex relationship since the 1898–1946 period of U.S. colonial rule, and much of the Philippines' history has been plagued by guerrilla warfare. After the United States took control of the Philippines at the end of the Spanish-American War, the anti-Spanish nationalist resistance movement continued to violently resist U.S. rule. After a bloody counterinsurgency campaign, the United States emerged victorious in 1902. But despite tamping down the Philippine nationalist resistance, the United States never fully quelled resistance throughout its new territorial holding. In particular, it fought a brutal campaign against the Muslim Moro population in the southern Philippines.

In 1935, the United States granted the self-governing commonwealth status, with a plan put in place to transition the country to full independence in 1945. But in the meantime, the Philippines became a key World War II location in the Pacific theater. In 1942, Japan occupied the islands, controlling the Philippines until the United States, fighting alongside Filipino resistance forces, began to reclaim control from the Japanese in 1944 and regained control of the islands in 1945. Many Filipinos welcomed the U.S. military role fighting the Japanese occupation. Following Japan's surrender, the Republic of the Philippines attained independence in July 1946. A democratic government was elected to coincide with national independence. Manuel Roxas was elected the country's first president in 1946. Armed insurgencies almost immediately threatened the postindependence government. Most threatening was the Hukbalahap, or Huk, a communist insurgency that began its rebellion against the Roxas government in 1946 and was not defeated until 1954.

The United States played a significant role in the Philippines following its independence. This role was not confined to helping counter the Huk insurgency. The Philippine government, under President Roxas, approved a "Military Bases Agreement" in 1947. It gave the United States the right to establish military bases and other installations, which, in turn, meant that U.S. troops would have access to the Philippines. The Government of the Republic of the Philippines (GRP)–U.S. Mutual Defense Agreement followed in 1952 to provide a security umbrella and military assistance to the Philippine government. The agreement remained in place after Philippine president Ferdinand Marcos—a close Cold War ally of the United States—declared martial law in 1972, and it remained an important mechanism for the United States to funnel aid to the regime until Marcos was deposed in 1986. After Marcos, the Philippines transitioned to democracy. U.S.-GRP relations were fragile, however, and when the U.S.-GRP basing agreement expired in 1991, the Philippine Congress voted for the closure of Clark Air Base and U.S. Naval Base Subic Bay—two of the largest U.S. military bases outside the continental United States. Following the closure of the bases in 1992, U.S.-Philippine security cooperation diminished dramatically until ratification of the Visiting Forces Agreement (VFA) in 1999 (Watts et al., 2014, pp. 66–67).

Throughout this period, conflict had continued in the restive southern Philippines, which is culturally distinct from the rest of the heavily Catholic country. Most of the 5 percent of the population who are Moro Muslim or belong to other indigenous groups are concentrated in several provinces of the Mindanao island group. Heavy resettlement of Christians from the Visayas and Luzon island groups to the north dating to the colonial period had exacerbated poverty, discrimination, and tensions. The Moro National Liberation Front (MNLF) formed in 1969 as an armed organization promoting a separate Moro Muslim state. The MNLF had some 30,000 armed fighters in the 1970s, but their numbers dwindled as successive Philippine governments conducted both military operations and initiated peace talks. After a first cease-fire accord was reached in 1976, some rebels rejected the talks and formed a splinter group, the Moro Islamic Liberation Front (MILF). In 1989, the Philippine government established the Autonomous Region in Muslim Mindanao (ARMM) and offered limited autonomy in several provinces, and, in 1996, the government signed a peace accord with the MNLF.

## Multiple Threat Groups

Despite its peace efforts, the Republic of the Philippines continued to face multiple insurgencies and terrorist threats and organizations.[1] By the late 1990s, the Philippines' main internal threats were the New People's Army (NPA), a communist insurgency that is active throughout the country though primarily in the north; the MILF, an Islamist-separatist movement that is active in the south; and another more radical Islamist splinter group, the ASG, which appeared on the scene in 1991.

The ASG, a Salafi jihadist organization based in the southern provinces of Basilan and Sulu, developed links to al Qaeda (AQ) during the 1990s, when members traveled to Afghanistan and received funding from Osama bin Laden.[2] The ASG's estimated number of members increased significantly throughout the 1990s, from 120 in 1993 to at least 1,270 in 2000 by Armed Forces of the Philippines (AFP) estimates, and over 2,000 by U.S. government estimates.[3] The group's armed activity increased over the mid- to late 1990s, including 36 attacks in 1995 and 29 in 1999.

This period of ASG growth and armed activity overlaps with the period in which AQ operatives were most active in the country, including the unsuccessful plotting of the so-called Bojinka attacks

---

[1] For in-depth case studies of these organizations, see Human Development Network, 2005.

[2] Indeed, the ASG was named for the former Afghan mujahedeen commander, Abdul Rasul Sayyaf, who trained foreign militants in his camps (Abuza, 2005, pp. 3–8).

[3] Data from the office of the Deputy Chief for Intelligence, J-2, AFP. The U.S. State Department's Patterns of Global Terrorism report for 2000 estimates the ASG's size at more than 2,200 (U.S. Department of State, 2001).

in 1995 by Ramzi Yousef and his uncle, the 9/11 mastermind Khalid Sheikh Mohammed. From their rented Manila apartment, Yousef and Mohammed developed the extremely ambitious Bojinka plots, in which Muslim attackers would assassinate Pope John Paul II and hijack 11 airliners and fly them into various targets, including the U.S. Central Intelligence Agency's HQ in Langley, Virginia. The Philippines was also an important hub for AQ financing. During the 1990s, for example, Osama bin Laden's brother-in-law and senior AQ financier Mohammed Jamal Khalifa used Philippine front companies and charities to support the Bojinka plots, as well as the ASG, the local Islamic jihadi group.[4]

The United States did not prioritize terrorist threats in the Philippines during the 1990s, but this began to change in 2000 and in 2001—before the 9/11 attacks—as a result of ASG kidnappings of U.S. citizens, holding them for ransom, and a demonstrated willingness to kill them.

This interest was limited, coming primarily from 1st Special Forces Group (SFG) (Airborne), 1st Battalion (BN), out of Okinawa, Japan. In March 2001, Company B, 1st BN, 1st SFG, out of Okinawa, began training the first AFP light reaction company (LRC) following a string of ASG kidnappings of U.S. hostages who were held for ransom. First, the ASG took an American Muslim, Jeffrey Schilling, hostage on Jolo Island on August 29, 2000, and held him for seven and a half months before releasing him. U.S. concerns about limited counterterrorist capabilities in the Philippines heightened further in May 2001, when ASG assailants kidnapped two U.S. missionaries, Gracia and Martin Burnham, and another U.S. citizen, Guillermo Sobero, from the Dos Palmas Resort in Palawan. The ASG captors, led by Abu Sabaya ("Bearer of Captives") whisked them hundreds of miles by boat to the ASG stronghold of Basilan, where they were held in captivity (Bowden, 2007). Sobero's captors beheaded him on June 11, 2001, calling it a "birthday present" to President Gloria Macapagal Arroyo on

[4] Several interviewees suggested that the increase in ASG size during this period can be at least partly attributed to the increase in resources it enjoyed courtesy of foreign terrorist organizations. For example, interview 60, October 29, 2014; interview 40, October 11, 2014.

the 103rd anniversary of Emilio Aguinaldo's declaration of Philippine independence from Spain. Sabaya tried—unsuccessfully—to distribute video footage of the Sobero beheading to Philippine media outlets but found no takers (interview 60, October 29, 2014). At that point, the high-profile nature of the kidnappings made hostage rescue, and Philippine counterterrorist capabilities more generally, a higher priority for the U.S. government.

Throughout the 2000s, the foreign terrorist organization with which the ASG maintained the strongest direct linkages, including operational linkages, was Indonesia's JI. The ASG was equally well known for its high-profile criminal activities, including kidnap-for-ransom operations targeting Westerners. None of the groups posed an existential threat to the GRP. They did, however, foment widespread instability, undermine foreign investment, participate in rampant human trafficking, and engage in subregional terrorism.

## Pre–Operation Enduring Freedom—Philippines Decision to Support the Light Reaction Company

Even examples of pre-9/11 terrorist threats emanating from the Philippines, such as Bojinka and the Burnham kidnappings, initially drew only limited interest from the U.S. government. Then-MAJ Joseph Felter, a Special Forces (SF) officer who, in 1999, was assigned to the U.S. Embassy in Manila as a military attaché, viewed the lack of PSF capabilities to conduct counterterrorist operations, including hostage rescue, as a significant threat to U.S. interests. Felter had a close relationship with AFP SOF from deployments to the Philippines as an SF operational detachment—alpha (ODA) team leader in the 1990s. As one of the few U.S. officials who spent considerable time in the southern Philippines following the reduction of the military-to-military relationship and a U.S. Department of Defense (DoD) embassy officer who viewed the kidnappings and threat to Americans in the Philippines from a close vantage point, Felter believed that the AFP could conduct missions, such as hostage rescue—but not without increased capacity, which the United States could provide (interview 66, November 7, 2014). Felter briefed then–State Department CT coordinator Michael A. Sheehan, who was visiting the Philippines, on the potential benefit of assisting the GRP in building a PSF CT capability, which led to U.S. military assistance to support the AFP's stand-up of an elite counterterrorist unit called the LRC (interview 66, November 7, 2014; Sheehan, 2008, p. 123).

The 2000 incidents, along with other events, influenced U.S. government officials, led by Ambassador Sheehan, to advocate for the development of a Philippine military national counterterrorist capability. In September 2000, a USPACOM planning team led by ADM Dennis C. Blair with members of SOCPAC, the Joint U.S. Military Assistance Group (JUSMAG) to the Republic of the Philippines, and the 1st SFG (Airborne) met with Philippine military and government officials in Manila to begin planning for an extensive mobile training team mission under Title 22 Chapter 22 (Mutual Security Assistance) authorities to organize, train, and equip this new force for the AFP that would be called the LRC.

### Light Reaction Company Stand-Up

The 1st SFG, commanded by COL David Fridovich, assumed responsibility for training the LRC. U.S. SF planners, based on extensive long-term relationships with the AFP, particularly with Philippine SF and First Scout Ranger Regiment (1st SRR), developed the detailed equipment requirements and a six-month training program of instruction to provide a comprehensive CT capability for rural and urban situations. The program included urban and rural tactical training, assault of multiple structures, communications, intelligence, medical training, and sniper operations. In March 2001, Company B, 1st Bn, 1st SFG, based in Okinawa, arrived in the Philippines to begin training the first AFP LRC (interview 45, October 16, 2014; interview 60, October 29, 2014).

On May 27, 2001, members of the ASG carried out the Dos Palmas kidnapping on Palawan Island and brought the hostages to Basilan Island at the southern tip of Mindanao. The Philippine military initially wanted to stop training and deploy the LRC to Basilan in support of operations to rescue the hostages, but the AFP eventually agreed that the LRC's training should be completed before the unit was deployed.

The LRC completed training in early July and was immediately sent to Basilan, where the ASG had regrouped after the Dos Palmas kidnappings. The LRC received good training and equipment from its 1st Bn, 1st SFG advisers, but the unit lacked a clear command-and-control (C2) structure when it deployed to Basilan. The 1st Bn, 1st SFG soldiers who trained the first LRC recommended that U.S. SOF advisers deploy to Basilan to assist the unit as it continued its initial stand-up, but their recommendation was rejected.

The LRC was deployed to Basilan on its inaugural operation, and, perhaps unsurprisingly, the commanders on the ground did not appropriately employ it. Instead of employing the LRC in missions for which it was trained, i.e., as the lead assault element in the hostage-rescue operation and other direct-action raids, the battle-space owner used other units as the assault force and employed the LRC to cordon the objective's perimeter during raids (interview 60, October 29, 2014; interview 66, November 7, 2014; interview 46, October 21, 2014; interview 45, October 16, 2014; interview 49, November 13, 2014; interview 61, October 31, 2014).[5]

During these initial operations, another major deficiency became obvious: the lack of a C2 mechanism to integrate the LRC with the regional command in Mindanao. U.S. SF, as part of SOCPAC's Pacific Situation Assessment Team at the embassy in Manila, kept in close contact with the leadership of the LRC on Basilan and confirmed the concerns of the trainers. Throughout the summer of 2001, SOCPAC and USPACOM monitored the situation and decided that a thorough assessment was needed to determine further training requirements for the LRC and the AFP.

In order to explore the opportunities to continue assisting the LRC, the commander of 1st Bn, 1st SFG, LTC David Maxwell, was tasked to meet with the LRC leadership in Mindanao on September 11, 2001. The attacks in New York and Washington resulted in

---

[5] AFP SOF soldiers agreed that the LRC was misused initially on Basilan (interview 30, October 9, 2014; interview 39, October 11, 2014; interview 43, October 9, 2014).

the meeting's postponement for three days. Concurrently, Brig Gen Donald C. Wurster and 1st Group commander Colonel Fridovich proposed adding a terrorism coordination and assistance visit (TCAV) into a planning survey that was to be conducted prior to Exercise Balikatan 02-1, which was scheduled to begin in January 2002. Their Filipino counterparts agreed, and a preparatory visit was scheduled for September 12, 2001. The timing was purely serendipitous. The 9/11 attacks postponed that visit by a week, but conferred new urgency and meaning to the effort. The Philippines would become, in essence, the "second front" in the U.S. global war on terrorism.

CHAPTER THREE

# 2001–2004: The Initiation of Operation Enduring Freedom—Philippines

## U.S.-Philippine Policy Decisions

In the wake of the 9/11 attacks, Washington and Manila engaged in national-level dialogue about enhanced U.S. military engagement in the Philippines as part of the global war on terrorism. Philippine president Arroyo was among the first to offer support for the United States, and the two governments began discussions on increased levels of assistance and cooperation. At that time, rescuing the American hostages held by the ASG was a top priority for the United States. Initial U.S. proposals envisaged a direct combat role for U.S. military personnel, the commitment of elite special mission units to lead operations to rescue the Burnhams, and assistance to the AFP against the ASG. However, negotiations with the Philippines over the rules of engagement (ROE) for the Balikatan exercise resulted in a more limited U.S. role: Filipino officials insisted on a noncombat role for the Americans, operations against only the ASG, and a geographical limitation of U.S. operations to only Basilan Island and the Zamboanga peninsula (interview 59, November 13, 2014; interview 46, October 21, 2014; see also Niksch, 2007, pp. 10–12).

At USPACOM, Admiral Blair requested and received a variety of proposals. One proposed plan was to conduct an aggressive offensive to land forces on Basilan to clear the island of terrorist groups and rescue the U.S. hostages. Blair asked special operations officers for their views on the feasibility of this plan, as well as for a potential timeline for it to achieve the desired end state. They stated that a U.S.-led offensive operation might achieve short-term results but that it would be highly problematic for the Philippine government and that Asian countries might see it as widening the war to their region (interview 46, October 21, 2014; interview 45, October 16, 2014). Colonel Fridovich, with the support of SOCPAC commander Brigadier General Wurster, recommended a more deliberate approach in which U.S. forces would work by, through, and with the AFP to help build capacity to defeat the insurgents and terrorists while ensuring that the United States respected Philippine sovereignty and domestic law. When asked how long this approach might take, their response was that, with a sustained commitment, the situation could be improved in the next ten years. Blair visited the Philippines for consultations with senior officials in mid-November 2001.

A week later, U.S. president George W. Bush and Arroyo met in Washington to seal a deal. The United States designated the Philippines a major non–North Atlantic Treaty Organization ally upon the GRP's demonstrated support for the United States after the 9/11 attacks. As part of the agreement, U.S. security and development assistance increased dramatically. In 2001, the United States obligated $10.5 million in military assistance to the Philippines. In 2002, U.S. military assistance increased more than five-fold, to more than $56 million. Through 2010, the United States never obligated less than $34 million in military assistance to the Philippines.[1] Figure 3.1 shows the amount of military assistance the United States provided to the Philippines annually from 2000 to 2012. Assistance from the U.S. Agency for International Development (USAID), $47.4 million in 2001, almost doubled by 2007.[2] USAID and the Millennium Challenge Corporation provided most U.S. assistance; the majority of USAID assistance was directed to the southern Philippines to support economic development and the peace process. The largest program, Growth with Equity in Mindanao (GEM), totaled $180.9 million between 2002 and 2012. A follow-on grant of $127.7 million began in 2012 to support the Mindanao Peace and Development Program.

---

[1] These amounts are in real historical U.S. dollars, not constant rates.

[2] USAID assistance in 2007 was $82.8 million (USAID, 2015).

**Figure 3.1**
**U.S. Military Assistance to the Philippines, 2000–2012**

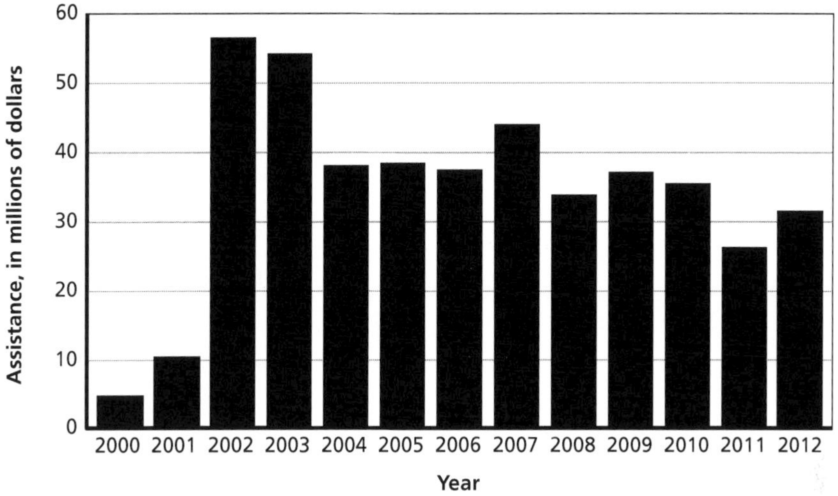


SOURCE: USAID, 2015.
RAND *RR1236-3.1*

## The Initial Assessment

While national-level negotiations were under way, the TCAV occurred in October and early November. The U.S. assessment, planning, and approval process took place from October 2001 to January 2002. Although it was a lengthy process in comparison to that which occurred prior to the post-9/11 U.S. deployment of troops to Afghanistan, this deliberate process permitted a thorough assessment of the environment and the partner force, which would continue to be updated throughout execution of the mission (Fridovich and Krawchuk, 2007). Four basic principles were developed from this initial study:

> First, the AFP and the Philippine government could benefit from the advice and assistance of U.S. military and other U.S. government agencies to overcome mutually agreed shortcomings. Second, U.S. forces had to work through and with AFP forces, with the AFP always in the lead with no unilateral or direct U.S.

> combat operations. Third, the U.S. forces had to ensure respect for the sovereignty of the Philippines and have a thorough understanding of the political environment and the sensitivities therein and conduct operations in ways that took those sensitivities into account. Fourth, the U.S. effort had to be joint and interagency and capable of being sustained for a long duration (years), and this in turn required continuous assessment. (Maxwell, 2011, pp. 7–8)

With Blair and Wurster's support, Fridovich, a career SF officer, took the lead as the TCAV assessment's primary architect. Fridovich's idea for the TCAV assessment grew out of his previous experiences in Bosnia and Haiti and as an observer/controller while detailed to the Joint Readiness Training Center. Another influence was a 1997 *Special Warfare* article by Kalev I. Sepp, "Preparing for 2010: Thinking Outside the Box" (Sepp, 1997, pp. 2–6). Sepp's article, which proved prescient in the wake of 9/11, began from the premise that, in the coming years, the United States would seek to maintain the existing nation-state system because the nature of the wars it would fight would be primarily unconventional, consisting of what was, at the time, called "operations other than war" (Sepp, 1997, p. 3). In such a scenario, Sepp argued, the use of military force would not always be appropriate, but the use of military forces would often be essential. SOF elements—particularly, U.S. SF, civil affairs (CA), and military information support operations (MISO)—would be critical to the increasingly joint force required to effectively fight these ambiguous, unconventional wars.[3]

Fridovich designed the assessment to cover the national, command, and local levels to arrive at a comprehensive view of the Philippine partners, as well as the physical, human, and enemy terrain in Basilan. "It was important that we go (to Basilan) so we could see what was really going on," Fridovich said. "We needed to see how the population there looked at us" (interview 46, October 21, 2014). But the assessment was more ambitious than simply collecting impressions of the local context. It was to be comprehensive, transparent, and data-

[3] In the article, Sepp made another prescient observation—that the term *operations other than war* would probably soon become doctrinally obsolete. See Sepp, 1997, pp. 4–5.

driven. Moreover, its findings would be shared widely with both U.S. and Filipino stakeholders as a basis for collaborative decisionmaking. Finally, the assessment would form a baseline on which to build future assessments and evaluate the progress of the campaign (interview 46, October 21, 2014).

In October 2001, Fridovich's TCAV team, which included Army, Navy, and Air Force special operations personnel, as well as intelligence officers and an embassy representative, deployed to the Philippines to begin the assessment. Fridovich needed, and managed to gain, GRP and AFP cooperation, including access to sensitive information from the GRP and AFP, in order to conduct the top-to-bottom assessment of the situation at the strategic, operational, and tactical levels. The TCAV team coordinated with the U.S. embassy and was given access to the AFP. It reviewed strategic documents and held meetings with senior officials to get their views on the terrorist threat on Basilan.

In the southern Philippines, AFP U.S. Southern Command (SOUTHCOM) commander LTG Roy Cimatu was key to the assessment's success. (At the time, SOUTHCOM was the command responsible for all of the southern Philippines.) Cimatu understood the utility of the assessment and supported Fridovich's team by granting access to his staff, as well as to brigades (BDEs) and BNs on Basilan, including the 1st Infantry Division Command and the forward (FWD) C2 HQ, TF Comet (interview 46, October 21, 2014; Maxwell, 2011). The TCAV team visited these units three or four days in a row, which was significant because U.S. forces had not visited Basilan since the ASG had been holding hostages there.

Each night, the TCAV team gathered to put together the data collected during the day. The results of the assessment demonstrated the need for more-capable PSF and for PSF to strengthen their relationship with the local population. AFP units deployed to SOUTHCOM generally had poor or limited relations with the population and thus had little access to ASG and JI areas without resorting to using heavy force to gain it. Another of the TCAV's important findings was that the Philippine government had never asked the majority of the population about its basic needs. This presented an opportunity to win over key segments of the population by addressing the basic needs identified in the assessment (Lambert, Lewis, and Sewall, 2012, pp. 123–124). Other findings included a lack of AFP capacity to conduct CT operations: AFP forces in the areas visited generally possessed a poor communication structure, limited mobility and logistics capabilities, and poor intelligence fusion capabilities, which are critical for effective CT operations (Briscoe, 2004b, p. 17).

The TCAV team quickly began sending reports back to SOCPAC. The findings suggested an approach that took shape quickly. The TCAV team briefed the findings to Cimatu's full staff—an audience of approximately 40 colonels, according to Fridovich. Although some SOUTHCOM officers were unreceptive to the idea of a U.S. advise-and-assist mission—their common refrain was that they needed only U.S. equipment and technical assistance, not advising—General Cimatu appreciated Fridovich's assessment and was convinced that a U.S. advise-and-assist mission would help to improve security in the SOUTHCOM area of responsibility (AOR). To cultivate and maintain this support, Fridovich and Maxwell emphasized the importance of not treating AFP counterparts as "junior partners" in the planning and execution of the nascent effort. They believed that the surest way to lose Philippine support was to be perceived as a colonial power or to disrespect the limitations on what the U.S. military could do under the laws and constitution of the Philippines. "We told them we were there to do what they wanted to do," Fridovich said, to allay their concerns that the United States might act unilaterally (interview 46, October 21, 2014).

Having gained the support of key AFP stakeholders, the U.S. Embassy in Manila and USPACOM both expressed support for the Basilan plan. The TCAV's findings, delivered in November, convinced Blair that the Basilan operation should be conducted through the Philippine forces as recommended; he approved the plan in January and sent it to Washington. In the meantime, a small contingent was deployed to Cimatu's command as a fusion cell to support planning there.

## Joint Task Force 510 and the Terms of Reference

USPACOM activated JTF 510 to plan and prepare to implement the first phase of Operation Freedom Eagle as part of Exercise Balikatan 02-1 in January 2002. On February 2, 2002, chairman of the Joint Chiefs of Staff Gen Richard Myers directed that Operation Freedom Eagle be renamed OEF-P. Advance elements of JTF 510 began arriving in the Philippines in mid-January.

Upon arrival in the Philippines, Wurster immediately grasped the gravity of OEF-P's sensitivity in the Philippines. The prospect of U.S. troops deploying to a combat zone reawakened anti-American nationalism born of the long history of the U.S. military presence in the Philippines, which had ended with the U.S. withdrawal from Clark and Subic, as well as the U.S. support for the long-running Marcos dictatorship. The history also included liberation from Japanese occupation, intermarriage, and many positive elements, but a sizable group of politicians opposed the mission. Miriam Defensor Santiago, a longtime influential Philippine senator and one of the most-vocal critics of U.S. military presence, led an effort to ensure the adoption of strict ROE that would ensure Philippine sovereignty under the country's constitution.

On February 7, 2002, the Philippine Senate conducted a hearing to debate the terms of reference to which the U.S. and Philippine governments had agreed for holding this exercise in the combat area of the southern Philippines, particularly the activities that U.S. troops would undertake.

The terms of reference stipulated that the exercise would last for six months, and efforts would be targeted against the ASG on the island of Basilan, with further advising, assisting, and training exercises to be conducted in the Zamboanga area and air support based in Cebu. U.S. forces were not to engage in combat, with the exception of self-defense. The exercise would be implemented jointly by the GRP and the United States under the authority of the AFP chief of staff. U.S. forces were prohibited from operating independently. However, AFP and U.S. unit commanders were to retain command over their respective forces. No permanent basing or support facilities would be built, but temporary structures for billeting, classroom instruction, and messing could be set up for use by GRP and U.S. forces. U.S. forces were to receive a country and area briefing on the culture and sensitivities of the Filipinos and the provisions of the VFA prior to their deployment. U.S. and GRP forces were allowed to share resources, equipment, and other assets through their respective logistics channels. GRP and U.S. forces, in consultation with community and local government officials, would jointly plan and execute socioeconomic-assistance projects. These terms were controversial, but the Supreme Court of the Philippines eventually approved them as legal (quoted from *Lim v. Arroyo*, 2002).

At the same time that the terms of reference were being debated, USPACOM commander Blair was finalizing his instructions for the U.S. forces. The terms of reference were a bilateral agreement between the two countries, and Blair's "commander's guidance" constituted his formal orders to those under his command. Blair and Wurster worked to ensure that the guidance was completely consistent with the bilateral terms and clarified specifically how U.S. forces and equipment were to be used.

In a February 2002 letter responding to Blair's draft guidance, Wurster framed the situation thusly:

> I recommend that this document remain titled "Commander's Guidance" in light of the turmoil surrounding the Terms of Reference between me and the [GRP] leadership here. I would not want this document from you to be misconstrued as a "secret" terms of reference. There is no question about what the AFP and US intends to happen in the field here but the time required for appropriate review and coordination has led to media speculation with Congressional interest. Bottom line is: command follows national lines. Philippine commander's authority on the ground will not be infringed. Our soldiers will support the operational instructions of the commander in the field, in accordance with their mission statement from me. No unilateral US operations . . . as that seems to be the most sensitive issue here.

### Mission Statement and Commander's Intent

The mission statement for JTF 510 was finalized as follows: "When directed, JTF 510 conducts military operations to train, advise, and assist designated AFP forces to enhance their ability to combat terrorism in SOUTHCOM in support of Operation Enduring Freedom" (Wurster, undated).

Guidance for execution of the mission was fleshed out in JTF 510's commander's guidance. A draft commander's guidance statement from the commander in chief of USPACOM (USCINCPAC) to the commander of JTF 510, dated February 2, 2002, read,

> 1. This memorandum specifies my intent for Operation Freedom Eagle, and includes specific guidance on some of the more important aspects of the operation.
>
> 2. JTF-510 conducts military operations to train, advise, and assist designated AFP forces to enhance their ability to combat terrorism in SOUTHCOM in support of operation ENDURING FREEDOM. You will accomplish the mission using training activities and advisor support to the AFP Southern Command. The Security Assistance Program will simultaneously improve the maintenance of equipment of the AFP, enable limited infrastructure development through CMO, and provide formal programs of instruction for specific AFP units. JTF-510 will work with [the Joint U.S. Military Assistance Group] to ensure that security assistance in SOUTHCOM is integrated into an effective campaign targeting the defeat of the Abu Sayyaf Group in the southern Philippines.
>
> 3. The mission guidance in paragraph 2 is general and potentially open-ended. As you close phase one forces and begin to integrate advisors throughout SOUTHCOM command and control headquarters. I expect from you continuous planning to improve specific areas of AFP effectiveness in their effort against the ASG and other recognized terrorist groups in the SOUTHCOM AOR. Develop and present an overall plan that integrates proposed

> areas for improvement during subsequent activity. Sample areas include but are not limited to:
>
> - Fused operations and intelligence
> - Communications
> - Command-and-control
> - Mobility
> - Maintenance
> - Battalion, Company, and lower tactical skills. (Blair, 2002)

USCINCPAC made explicit that the AFP's SOUTHCOM was to be a key stakeholder and partner in implementing the guidance:

> Your recommendations for phase two should be coordinated to the maximum extent possible with Southern Command leadership. The plans should identify measures of effectiveness to serve as the basis for deciding when to end the mission. (Blair, 2002)

### Use of Enablers

USCINCPAC also described the use of U.S. and USPACOM assets that would be provided as key enablers of JTF 510.

#### *Intelligence, Surveillance, and Reconnaissance Support*

USCINCPAC's commander's guidance document noted, "fused intelligence is a known weakness of the Southern Command." In support of JTF 510's mission, he would assign USPACOM intelligence, surveillance, and reconnaissance (ISR) to support the AFP campaign but noted that it would be used only for targeting the recognized terrorist groups in the SOUTHCOM AOR. Before deploying ISR to support AFP CT efforts, however, he also requested assurance from Wurster that "it will feed into an improved Southern Command intelligence structure that can use it effectively" (Blair, 2002). In effect, Blair wanted confirmation, based on Wurster's in-theater assessment as JTF 510 commander, that support from valuable ISR assets would not be squandered and that Wurster's force would be able to help the AFP use it to enhance operational effectiveness. USPACOM did provide ISR assets, including the P-3 aircraft, which enhanced SOUTHCOM's operational capabilities and effectiveness. U.S. information-sharing and ISR support remained key enablers of AFP effectiveness and important sources of U.S. assistance throughout the entirety of OEF-P.

#### *Secure Communication Equipment*

One of the immediate benefits that the arrival of U.S. advisers had for the AFP's SOUTHCOM was JTF 510's secure communications. Blair authorized Wurster to make the capability of U.S. secure communication networks available to the AFP, so long as JTF 510 retained control of the equipment. Blair reminded Wurster, however, that part of the overall campaign plan was for the AFP to develop their own secure communication network (Blair, 2002).

#### *Mobility Platforms*

SOCPAC's pre-mission assessments had also found that the AFP lacked the mobility capabilities to conduct operations, as well as to evacuate casualties. JTF 510 was authorized to use its air, land, and sea platforms to transport AFP members, as well as its own personnel. JTF 510 helicopters could be used for medical evacuation (MEDEVAC), quick-reaction forces (QRFs), and combat search and rescue (CSAR), provided they did not use hot landing zones.[4] Blair's guidance emphasized that the ultimate goal was for Philippine forces to provide these functions themselves: "The objective of the [security assistance]–funded maintenance program is for the AFP to improve the reliability and sustainment of its own helicopters to support Southern Command mobility." As with secure communications, JTF 510's support was intended to provide a short-term capability while JTF 510 advisers helped their AFP partners translate U.S.-provided security assistance into an independent, sustainable capability.

### Rules of Engagement

The final aspect of the commander's guidance concerned the ROE for JTF 510 in OEF-P. These reiterated the critical elements of the terms of reference to which the two countries agreed. First, the United States would not conduct unilateral operations. U.S. forces were to serve only as advisers and would not directly conduct any military actions.

[4] Paragraph 7 involved the deployment of a QRF under certain conditions.

Second, the AFP's chain of command would remain intact. U.S. advisers would offer their best professional advice, but AFP commanders would ultimately make operational decisions. U.S. advisers would respect these decisions. Third, the United States would retain a QRF capability and a CSAR capability. The QRF capability would enable the United States to ensure force protection for the JTF, and the CSAR would enable the United States to directly extract U.S. personnel from harm if they were to go missing (e.g., were captured and held hostage). The U.S. assets could also be used to evacuate Philippine casualties from casualty-collection points rather than from the battlefield itself.

### Balikatan 02-1 and the Beginning of Operation Enduring Freedom—Philippines

The legislative debate over OEF-P delayed the GRP's final approval of the terms of reference and the deployment of troops to Basilan until mid-February. To address nationalist sensitivities, the Philippine government had chosen to call the operation an exercise, Balikatan 02-1. Balikatan is the largest U.S.-Philippine joint exercise, which had been held in previous years in other parts of the Philippines. In effect, Balikatan 02-1 was the first phase of OEF-P.

JTF 510 deployed with 1,300 U.S. troops, which included 160 SOF personnel, to the Philippines in support of Balikatan 02-1. Of the total approved, only 600 personnel were permitted in the joint operational area of the southern Philippines. Because of a briefing error, the Philippine government changed the cap on forces in the southern Philippines at the last minute from 660 to 600, forcing Wurster to trim some HQ and other elements. The air units were based on Cebu. Air units were deployed from the 353rd Special Operations Group (SOG) and the 160th Special Operations Aviation Regiment. The primary ground units were 1st BN, 1st SFG (Airborne); one CA company; and, later in the spring, a naval construction task group (NCTG). A naval special warfare (NSW) unit and a boat detachment also deployed. During the initial infiltration, ten service members were killed when the MH-47 helicopter transporting them crashed on its return from Basilan to Cebu.

## U.S. Special Operations Forces Lines of Operation

The principal activities that JTF 510 carried out were CMO, information and intelligence gathering and sharing, and capacity-building and operational assistance to enable the AFP to conduct CT operations.

### *Civil–Military Operations*

CMO constituted a major component of OEF-P activities. These operations served multiple purposes: First, the activities enabled CA and other units conducting CMO to assess and gain a better understanding of the area, the population, and the enemy status. By learning about and then addressing basic population needs, the local population would typically become more receptive to the government. This receptivity could include a willingness to facilitate AFP access and operations. These operations included daylong events to provide the population in key areas with medical, dental, or veterinary care. Longer-term projects supplied and improved health facilities, schools, and water wells or pumps. Engineering units were brought in to construct, repair, or improve needed infrastructure.

These operations are designed to achieve both tactical and strategic objectives. They provide access and information to assist government forces in pursuing enemy forces. The strategic objectives include denying support and resources to adversaries. The population ideally becomes less hospitable to the enemy forces, which shrinks their support base, resources, and room for maneuver. Local community figures might also become more supportive of the government and hostile to the armed groups, further influencing local public opinion.

Many of the infrastructure projects served dual purposes. For example, the NCTG began improving the ring road around Basilan, which helped the local population get its crops to market and increased the mobility of AFP and JTF 510 forces to conduct military operations. The Basilan governor suggested that the JTF hire locals and supply hammers so they could pulverize rocks into gravel as part of the road-building project, thus providing steady work for thousands of residents (interview 59, November 13, 2014).

In the six months of Balikatan 02-1, U.S. and AFP units deployed to Basilan built 80 km of road, four bridges, two piers, and five water projects and treated 20,000 patients (JSOTF-P, 2007b, slide 8). These activities were underwritten by $2.2 million in humanitarian assistance funds and $4.5 million in USAID funds, as well as military operations and maintenance funds that could be used for dual-purpose projects that facilitated military operations or force protection. As part of the outreach to the population, MISO (formerly known as psychological operations [PSYOP]), though not conducted initially, were eventually employed. Military information support teams (MISTs) provided a range of services aimed at improving the target population's perceptions of the GRP's legitimacy and enhancing support for the rule of law. Activities included publicizing AFP CMO, advertising and facilitating the Rewards for Justice program, and helping the GRP convey the harm caused by transnational terrorist organizations.

#### *Intelligence Gathering and Sharing*

Both JTF 510 and JSOTF-P leveraged the technical superiority of the United States in OEF-P, using ISR assets and capabilities to enable AFP operations, enhance force protection for U.S. forces, and support CMO. Although U.S. interviewees found that their Filipino counterparts had developed extensive human intelligence (HUMINT) networks, U.S. ISR validated and supplemented that intelligence to find and "fix" terrorist targets that enabled PSF to conduct operations to "finish" them, and helped to improve decisionmaking by providing persistent situational awareness at key locations and times.

The United States deployed a variety of ISR platforms, initially relying primarily on the P-3 aircraft (JSOTF-P, 2008a; interview 59, November 13, 2014). In the first period, JTF 510 forces also deployed tactical unmanned aerial vehicles (UAVs). Unlike in Iraq and Afghanistan, U.S. forces in the Philippines lacked legal authority to conduct lethal operations, including operations employing armed UAVs. Unarmed UAVs and other collection systems were used extensively, however, both to aid AFP targeting and to provide force protection for U.S. forces. As in Afghanistan, Iraq, and other countries, host-nation demand for U.S. ISR support in the Philippines was a significant source of leverage the United States enjoyed vis-à-vis its host-nation counterpart.

ISR support was initially a sensitive issue given the overall sensitivity of the U.S. advisory mission in Mindanao. Ambassador Francis J. Ricciardone, who presented his credentials as chief of the U.S. mission in the Philippines just as Balikatan 02-1 was beginning, engaged with senior Philippine officials to assuage these and other concerns. He arranged a demonstration of the UAV platforms at the U.S. Embassy in Manila for President Arroyo and her defense secretary. He said,

> We recognized how sensitive it would be so our role was to show the Filipinos how it would work, what the control room would look like, and the [operations and intelligence] fusion that they would be part of. We flew these little handheld UAVs for them at the embassy in a demonstration. That way, the president and minister of defense felt they were adequately informed. (interview 65, December 19, 2014)

Throughout his tenure as ambassador from 2002 to 2005, Ricciardone remained actively involved with the strategic aspects of OEF-P. He kept President Arroyo apprised of U.S. activities, arranged high-level access for the TF as needed, and visited the southern Philippines with GRP leaders.

### *Capacity-Building and Operational Assistance*

JTF 510 provided advice and assistance both to AFP SOF and conventional forces. Because the capacity-building was explicitly aimed at achieving the CT objective of OEF-P, the efforts focused on Philippine special operations units, as well as conventional forces, deployed to the southern Philippines. U.S. operational advisory assistance and intelligence-sharing was authorized only with regard to the ASG or JI. The AFP capabilities that the TF helped develop were inherently fungible, and the GRP could and did use them to confront other threats.

#### Armed Forces of the Philippines Special Operations Forces

The AFP SOF units with which U.S. forces primarily worked during OEF-P were the LRC; the 1st SRR, a light infantry unit of approximately 1,800 AFP troops that was designed similarly to the U.S. Army's 75th Ranger Regiment; the SF Regiment (Airborne), which consists of approximately 1,200 personnel trained in unconventional warfare and counterinsurgency—the AFP's SF Regiment (Airborne) was designed to perform missions similar to those of the U.S. SF; and, finally, the AFP's CA Group, which evolved from the AFP's Public Relations Office of the 1950s and consists of more than 100 personnel trained in CMO (Farris, 2009, p. 22).

#### Armed Forces of the Philippines Conventional Forces

JTF 510 also invested significant time in advising and assisting AFP conventional forces operating under the joint unified HQ SOUTHCOM (which later split into two commands, WestMinCom and Eastern Mindanao Command [EastMinCom]). SOUTHCOM commanded elements of the Philippine Army, Air Force, Marine Corps, and Navy assigned to conduct operations in the southern Philippines. During Balikatan 02-1 and the first phase of OEF-P, most of the training and advising focused on 15 AFP Marine Corps and Army BNs deployed to Basilan. The advisory activities spanned the echelons from the three-star SOUTHCOM to the division, BDE, and BN commands. U.S. SOF were permitted to train tactical units but not accompany them on operations. The NSW component of JSOTF-P trained and advised both Philippine conventional navy and Naval SOG (NAVSOG) units in maritime interdiction operations and other missions and skills. U.S. Air Force Special Operations Command (AFSOC) personnel, as well as other U.S. airmen, provided a wide range of training and assistance to the Philippine Air Force (PAF), as detailed in Chapter Five.

### *Relationships Between Joint Task Force 510 and U.S. Southern Command*

Figure 3.2 outlines the task organization and relationship of JTF 510 with its AFP counterparts. Red lines denote coordination and synchronization nodes at each level of AFP command to provide advice and assistance.

JTF 510 advised and supported SOUTHCOM, and 1st Bn, 1st SFG advised JTF Comet, the AFP TF command on Basilan. The SF companies, or advanced operational bases (AOBs), were collocated with the BDE HQ. The subordinate SF teams, or ODAs, were assigned to advise and assist each Philippine Army and Marine Corps

**Figure 3.2**
**Joint Task Force 510 Task Structure for Its Advise-and-Assist Relationship with the Armed Forces of the Philippines**

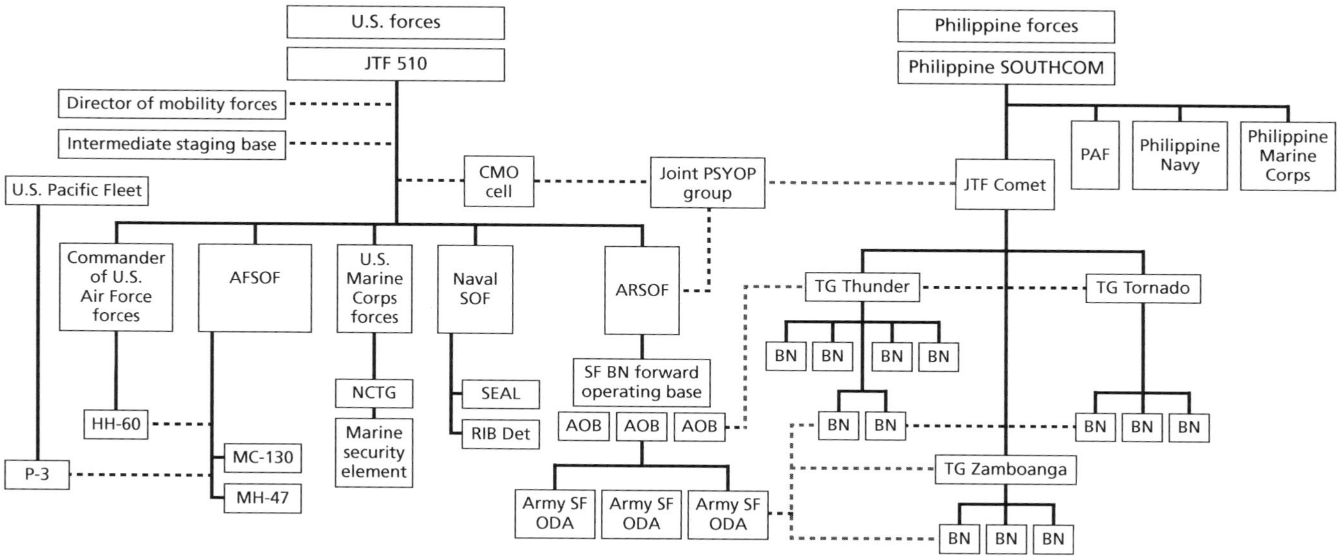


SOURCE: Wurster, undated.
NOTE: AFSOF = Air Force SOF. ARSOF = Army SOF. SEAL = sea, air, and land (U.S. Navy SOF). RIB = rubberized inflatable boat. Det = detachment. RIB Det is a naval special boat detachment equipped with 11-m RIBs. AOB = advanced operational base. HH-60 = HH-60 Pave Hawk helicopter. MC-130 = MC-130 aircraft. MH-47 = MH-47 Chinook helicopter. TG = task group. Red lines denote coordination and synchronization nodes at each level of AFP command to provide advice and assistance.
RAND *RR1236-3.2*

BN to conduct capacity-building, as well as to advise and assist during combat operations (Wurster, undated; interview 59, November 13, 2014). ODAs were also assigned to advise Scout Ranger Bns, LRCs, and Civilian Armed Forces Geographical Units.

## Key Joint Task Force 510 Operations

### *Operation Liberty*

After establishing rapport with their assigned units at rudimentary base camps, the SOF met with local government officials and began to conduct detailed assessments of barangays and municipalities. The resulting information was used to develop follow-on civic-action and engineering plans. In March and April, the AFP conducted Operation Liberty, for which the U.S. forces provided advisory, communications, medical, and ISR support. U.S. forces also supported exfiltration of surrendering fighters. The advisers determined particular shortfalls in reconnaissance, small-unit patrolling and first aid capability, and over-reliance on unconfirmed HUMINT, as well as the use of unobserved artillery fire; weapons and ammunition were seen to be in poor condition. All of these were the focus of subsequent training, as were tactical decisionmaking, intelligence preparation of the battlefield, marksmanship, and weapon repair and maintenance.

### *The Burnham Rescue*

Efforts to locate the Burnhams were plagued by rivalries among the Philippine Army and Marine Corps units on Basilan, with each hoping to be the one to locate the hostages. In addition, some collusion between the ASG and local sympathizers was also suspected. In the end, the marines found the Burnhams, but, in the rescue attempt, one of the American hostages, Martin Burnham, and a Filipino nurse were killed. Burnham's wife Gracia was shot in the leg but was successfully rescued. Basilan's difficult terrain, the guerrillas' familiarity with the area, and the OEF-P ROE at the time further complicated the challenging task. U.S. SOF trained units that eventually found the hostages, but they could not accompany commanders into the field to advise them on the rescue operation.

### *Targeting Abu Sabaya*

After the Burnham operation, JTF 510 supported numerous operational successes against terrorist networks targeting high-value individuals. The most important of these targets was ASG spokesman Abu Sabaya, who was one of the captors of the Burnhams and the others whom the ASG kidnapped from the resort in Dos Palmas. Sabaya, who, at the time, was the group's main public face, had risen to the ranks of the ASG's senior leadership. He loved the spotlight, and he drew attention to the Burnham hostage crisis through extensive outreach to Philippine media sources both in Mindanao and in Manila. In response, the U.S. government placed a $5 million reward for his arrest.

The AFP pursuit of Abu Sabaya entailed intelligence and combat operations by land and maritime forces, supported by JTF 510 operational advice, imagery intelligence (IMINT), ISR assets, and secure communication equipment (Bowden, 2007). The TF helped formulate and execute the plan to pursue Sabaya with support from AFSOC and NSW units (interview 65, December 15, 2014). In the operation, the Philippine Navy began by following a boat from a coastal village after an informant tipped them off about when and where Abu Sabaya would try to move to his Basilan hideout (Bowden, 2007). U.S. surveillance assets and Navy SEALs and boat crews accompanying Philippine forces helped track the 25-foot motorized Kingfisher outrigger canoe in which Sabaya was riding. The Philippine forces, who were using night-vision goggles (NVG), decided to intercept the boat after they saw seven armed men on board. As they approached, the soldiers received fire and shot back, hitting three men, who fell overboard. The Philippine forces' boat overran the other vessel, badly damaging it. The four other gunmen surrendered. A Philippine commando fired from short range at one rebel in a black sweatshirt who was trying to swim away—he was later confirmed, through deoxyribonucleic acid (DNA) evidence, to be Abu Sabaya.[5]

---

[5] After Sabaya's boat sank, two American MH-47 Chinook helicopters assisted in the search for the bodies of the guerrillas who had leaped overboard (Bowden, 2007).

## 2003–2004: Transition to Joint Special Operations Task Force—Philippines

After completing operations in the late summer of 2002, JTF 510 departed Zamboanga. The conclusion of Balikatan 02-1 and the departure of JTF 510 ushered in a period of uncertainty and adjustment for the U.S. SOF mission in the southern Philippines. Efforts to agree on a next phase of operations did not reach fruition. President Arroyo and SOUTHCOM commander General Cimatu were both in favor of a follow-on mission to the island of Jolo with a residual force that continued training through security assistance programs. Wurster kept AOB 170 and four SF ODA teams on Basilan as an overwatch to ensure the continuation of CMO and development efforts and to continue training the AFP through security assistance programs (interview 59, November 13, 2014). In late 2002, a joint SOTF (JSOTF) was formed; its mission was declared to be "foreign internal defense in order to enable the GRP to defeat terrorist groups in the Philippines" (JSOTF-P, 2002; JSOTF-P, undated [b], slide 4).[6] JSOTF-P's total manning was to be 226. The following year, JSOTF-P relocated to Manila, leaving a SOUTHCOM liaison element to continue advising and assisting the AFP command in Mindanao.[7]

ASG armed activity continued. On October 2, 2002, the ASG conducted a bombing in Zamboanga, which killed three people, including a U.S. SF soldier, in a joint operation with two Indonesian JI militants, as well as a Jordanian resident of the Philippines who was reportedly linked to the Palestinian terrorist group Hamas. ASG leader Khadaffy Janjalani oversaw the operation. This attack explicitly targeted U.S. forces and signaled a shift in the group's tactics—this was the group's first bombing since 1994 (interview 61, October 31, 2014).

---

[6] The briefing itself is undated, but the file is dated February 7, 2003.

[7] The SOUTHCOM liaison element was located on Edwin Andrews Air Base and left behind only one ODA in the southern Philippines, a dramatic drawdown from the strength of JTF 510 (interview 61, October 31, 2014).

### The Aborted Stand-Up of Joint Task Force 555

Eager to build on the successes of JTF 510 and Balikatan 02-1, President Arroyo endorsed her defense minister's idea for a follow-on mission in Jolo, the main island of Sulu province, which would include U.S. participation in direct combat in combined operations. USPACOM handed its U.S. Marine Corps component command the responsibility for planning the mission in early 2003. On January 21, 2003, U.S. Air Force Brig Gen Gregory L. Trebon replaced General Wurster as SOCPAC commander. On February 3, the USPACOM commander designated the Marine Corps component command as JTF-555, with responsibility for conducting the follow-on mission.

The robust plan developed by the Marine Corps envisioned some 1,000 U.S. forces engaging in combat operations alongside AFP forces on Jolo and Tawi-Tawi. As these plans became known in the Philippines, a political outcry ensued over the apparent U.S. intent to conduct combat operations in the Philippines. The public opposition forced President Arroyo to backtrack on her previous support for U.S. participation in combat. Negotiations continued, but, in the end, the GRP never approved terms of reference for JTF-555, and JTF-555 never deployed because of the failure to agree on its role. On March 3, 2003, Arroyo delayed execution of Balikatan 03-1 indefinitely, citing a constitutional ban on U.S. forces engaging in such actions (Hendren and Paddock, 2003). As he transitioned out, Wurster had watched the developing plans with skepticism; based on his experience in 2002, particularly the intense debate over the advisory ROE for JTF 510, he doubted that U.S. participation in direct combat in the Philippines would be tenable politically (interview 59, November 13, 2014).

During this period, the GRP permitted U.S. SOF to continue to provide training and assistance under JSOTF-P, which was based in Manila and commanded by U.S. Air Force Col Douglas R. Lengenfelder, its first commander. On April 1, 2003, CAPT David Pittelkow, who had previously commanded NSW Group 1, replaced Lengenfelder. U.S. Army LTC Dennis Downey then assumed command, to be followed in July 2004 by U.S. Army LTC Thomas M. Johnson, who served the first year-long tour as JSOTF-P commander until July 2005. Downey, a 1st SFG (Airborne) officer, served multiple tours in the Philippines, maintaining relationships and continuity through this period.

According to interviewees, the U.S. effort in the Philippines entered a less active period for several reasons, foremost of which were the ongoing negotiations over the scope of future U.S. involvement. Another factor was SOCPAC's adjustment to a more regional focus in this time period. Wurster's replacement, General Trebon, focused more on establishing military liaison elements throughout the region than the Philippines specifically (interview 46, October 21, 2014; interview 59, November 13, 2014). The brief tours of the JSOTF-P commanders during this time period also limited their ability to have a sustained impact or to engage in long-range planning. The U.S. SOF footprint reached its lowest point in the entire decade when JSOTF-P shrank to between 50 and 80 troops in 2004 (interview 46, October 21, 2014; interview 60, October 29, 2014; interview 59, November 13, 2014; interview 61, October 31, 2014).

### *The Continuation of U.S. Security Assistance and Joint Special Operations Task Force—Philippines Support*

During 2003 and 2004, two important activities continued during this relatively fallow period, however. The ongoing security assistance program provided mobile training teams through joint combined exchange training (JCET) to continue the training, equipping, and expansion of the Philippine SOF forces. Second, a small advisory effort continued in the southern Philippines via operations and intelligence fusion teams (OIFTs).

The security assistance that the United States provided to the Philippines focused on CT capabilities. Per a February 2003 JSOTF-P briefing to AFP chief of staff Angelo Reyes, JSOTF-P supported five U.S. security assistance modules: LRC training; night-vision aviation training; the stand-up of a new operations and intelligence fusion center; light-infantry BN training; and formal schooling for an NCO team leader course. Importantly, the operations and intelligence center would be located at SOUTHCOM HQ, where collocated JSOTF-P personnel could support AFP operations and intelligence fusion (JSOTF-P, 2002, pp. 1–4).[8]

This security assistance, authorized under the U.S. embassy's ongoing security cooperation programs, would provide sustainment to the original LRC as a future training cadre and to train two new LRCs; a trained BN HQ element that would provide national-level C2; and needed equipment, such as NVGs, secure communications, and appropriate weapons. Approximately 50 U.S. personnel served as advisers for the LRC's sustainment and development. For nighttime aviation, 14 U.S. forces, six of whom were from AFSOC's 6th Special Operations Squadron, were to train 24 AFP crewmembers, split between eight pilots, eight copilots, and eight crewmembers. U.S. advisers were tasked with training UH-1 crews to fly at night; to perform 24-hour casualty evacuation (CASEVAC) and MEDEVAC; and to provide support to ground forces during nighttime operations.

Other security cooperation activities also continued at this time. Another training effort focused on increasing the Philippine forces' ability to fuse operations and intelligence. The U.S. forces would provide equipment and expertise to a central, 60-person fusion center at SOUTHCOM HQ. This center would enhance higher-level planning at SOUTHCOM HQ and communications with five critical BDEs across the SOUTHCOM AOR.

### *Expanded Joint Special Operations Task Force—Philippines Advisory and Assistance in Central Mindanao*

Although the scope of JSOTF-P's advisory remained limited, the small force did direct its energies toward the migrating threat. However, in response to ASG and JI movement to central Mindanao after being squeezed from Basilan in 2002, JSOTF-P was able to establish in

[8] The cost estimates of these modules was $25 million, with $10 million directed to LRC training, $1.4 million to NVG aviation, $1.2 million to the operations and intelligence fusion center, $8.6 million to the light-infantry BNs, and $515,000 to the NCO team leaders' course. For equipment, $4.6 million was for AFP tactical secure communications, to be split among the light-infantry BN, LRC, and PAF (NVG aviation UH-1 kits); $3.5 million was provided for weapons, including the purchase of M4s and M1911 firearms, along with $2 million for U.S. and AFP ammunition. Another $2.8 million was for night-vision equipment and secure communication equipment.

2004 an OIFT based north of General Santos City, which was led by ODA 116. The OIFT was established following an expanded JCET in General Santos City. The OIFT in central Mindanao liaised with the 6th Infantry Division, as well as two BDEs that were operating against ASG and JI elements located in and around Palimbang, the Daguma Mountains, and Liguasan Marsh. JSOTF-P ISR assets were important for identifying ASG and JI columns so that operations could be carefully planned and executed if feasible.

The OIFT was renamed the TF Mindanao Liaison Coordination Element (LCE) in late 2004. Eventually, this grew into TF Mindanao in 2005. The operational presence and activities in central Mindanao marked a subtle yet important early expansion of JSOTF-P from JTF 510's main effort on Basilan in 2002. PSF targeted ASG smuggling networks in the area and disrupted a JI-run bomb-making course in which Filipino Islamist militants were being taught how to make a variety of sophisticated bombs, including improvised explosive devices (interview 72, January 23, 2015; interview 37, October 10, 2014).

### U.S. Focus on the Abu Sayyaf Group and Jemaah Islamiyah and the Rationale for Its Focus

Despite the complex environment with a multitude of threats, the United States would remain focused only on those groups with transnational terrorist ties. OEF-P, as part of the global CT effort, operated under the authorization for use of military force that granted the U.S. military special authority to target terrorist organizations that belonged to, or had connections to, AQ. The ASG and the JI had demonstrated connections to AQ. Other insurgencies—importantly, in the Philippines, the NPA, which was and continues to be the GRP's primary internal threat—do not have such ties. Consequently, U.S. forces were restricted from providing any support to PSF forces tasked with counterinsurgency against the NPA. Of course, improved PSF capabilities could be and were applied against the NPA, albeit without the operational assistance of U.S. SOF.[9]

In addition, U.S. government policy supported the Philippine government's various efforts to negotiate cease-fires and peace accords with the MNLF and the MILF, including support for reintegration of former combatants and respect for terms that permitted MNLF to retain arms within certain designated areas and receive advance warning of military operations. This fact and the number of small factions made for a complex operating environment. Although the U.S. effort was strictly focused on groups with transnational terrorist ties—the ASG and JI, primarily—and steered clear of supporting any other operations, the web of familial, clan, and patronage ties, in addition to political sympathies, led some armed elements to provide support, sanctuary, and recruits for each other.

Although U.S. officers understood and accepted the prohibition on U.S. forces engaging in combat, many of them believed that the restriction on providing operational advisory support below the BN level impeded mission success. As Maxwell wrote in a 2002 report,

> rapport with the AFP is going to wane because there is a perception that the US forces are not willing to commit to advising and assisting at the lowest levels. Furthermore, until US SF conducts advisory operations at the lowest tactical levels, [AFP] operations will never be sufficiently improved to get the job done. (Maxwell, 2002)

Although JTF 510 advisers were able to accompany BN commanders to the field, Maxwell judged this activity insufficient to remedy the tactical-level deficits.

JTF 510 eventually received permission to advise at the company level, but the ROE were modified too late to be of use in this period. President Arroyo had voiced her support for this shift well before the Pentagon finally granted these authorities. The rules changed after

---

[9] These frustrations were not limited to the Filipinos. U.S. SF have a history with the NPA—it is the group that assassinated SF COL James N. Rowe in 1989 (Maxwell, 2011, pp. 3–4).

Deputy Secretary of Defense Paul Wolfowitz visited the Philippines. He returned to Washington and secured authorization for U.S. forces supporting JTF 510 to operate at the company level (interview 59, November 13, 2014). However, this authorization was granted just two weeks before JTF 510 was scheduled to depart from the Philippines.

## Summary

The 2002–2004 period heralded the deployment of JTF 510, the Balikatan 02-1 exercise on Basilan, the initiation of the OEF-P campaign, and the transition of the large-scale 2002 mission to a smaller-scale security assistance and security cooperation effort. U.S. SOF conducted extensive assessments to gain an accurate and detailed understanding of the environment, enemy, and the population; they shared these assessments with the Philippine government and its forces. The training and equipping of Philippine forces and the operational assistance yielded initial operational effects on Basilan. CMO created greater access for U.S. and Philippine forces and enabled them to gain further information and understanding of the environment and the adversary.

The AFP, enabled by U.S. assistance, displaced the threat from Basilan and reduced conditions contributing to the threat. The U.S. SOF BN commander reported other indicators of a reduced-threat environment, including the return of some 1,000 displaced civilians and the resumption of public civic activities, such as a province-wide anniversary celebration and school graduations (Maxwell, 2002). Civilians' support for the U.S. presence was manifested in various ways, including resolutions of support passed by the Basilan Provincial Council and local barangay councils.[10] U.S. support, training, and preparation of AFP units enabled AFP hostage-rescue operations and counternet-

[10] Barangay councils, the most local form of government, were trusted by 66 percent of the population in six conflict-affected areas of Mindanao, including Basilan, just behind 71 percent who expressed trust in President Benigno Aquino (Teutsch and Thambidurai, 2014).

work operations. Extensive intelligence was provided through U.S. ISR assets.

The campaign to deny the ASG and JI sanctuary on Basilan disrupted their ability to conduct operations there and resulted in the degradation of ASG leadership, including a notable operation that resulted in the death of an ASG senior leader, Abu Sabaya, who was notorious for his role as the Burnhams' main captor (interview 46, October 21, 2014; interview 59, November 13, 2014).

As Figure 3.3 shows, enemy-initiated incidents on Basilan were steady in 2000, around 30, with an uptick in enemy-initiated incidents in 2001 caused by the fiercer combat, and a drop back to around 30 in 2002 to 2004. The number of government casualties encountered on Basilan dropped from 32 in 2000 to 12 in 2002 despite the heavier combat action. Government forces suffered only eight casualties in 2003.

**Figure 3.3**
**Enemy-Initiated Incidents in Basilan, Sulu, and Tawi-Tawi, 2000–2004**

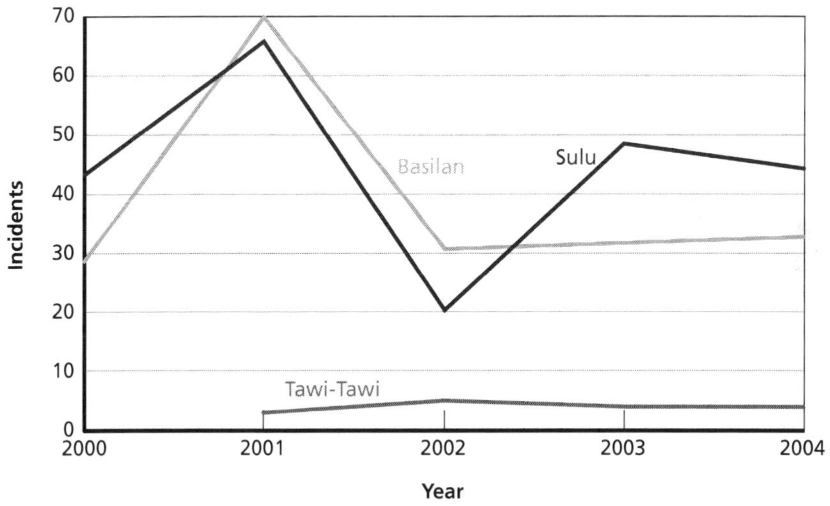


SOURCE: Empirical Studies of Conflict (ESOC) data.
NOTE: Incidents are counts of enemy-initiated incidents per year by province.
RAND *RR1236-3.3*

The success achieved during the initial years of OEF-P was primarily at the tactical and operational levels. U.S. advisers focused on basic military skills, such as combat patrols and marksmanship, which, however rudimentary, improved the AFP's capacity to find, fix, and finish the ASG. The U.S. intervention had helped to disrupt and degrade the terrorist networks on Basilan and to secure the island, at least temporarily. U.S. SOF understood that building Philippine capacity would take time. The defeat of the ASG would also not occur overnight; the threat had been displaced to central Mindanao and Sulu province.

CHAPTER FOUR

# 2005–2007: The Move to Jolo and Operation Ultimatum

Because of the upsurge in violence, President Arroyo was determined to take action. She ordered the deployment of Philippine Marine Corps to Jolo to confront the rising tide of attacks. In early 2005, Fridovich, newly installed as SOCPAC commander, spearheaded a new assessment that led to an indefinite extension of OEF-P authorities and U.S. advisory assistance to AFP units in the southern Philippines, including Jolo and elsewhere in the Sulu archipelago, as well as central Mindanao. Fridovich employed similar methods to those used on Basilan in 2002, as well as major operations, including complex amphibious landings, deception operations, and maritime interdiction operations. Executing this phase of OEF-P was JSOTF-P commander COL James B. Linder and his successor, Colonel Maxwell, who had led the early Basilan operations in 2002. Maxwell also oversaw a return to Basilan and the creation of TF Archipelago led by U.S. NSW units, which extended operational assistance on the island of Tawi-Tawi a few miles from Malaysia. Tawi-Tawi functioned primarily as a transit zone for fighters, facilitators, and resources, rather than a venue for attacks, as the attack data in Figure 3.3 in Chapter Three and Figure 4.2 indicate.

## Assessment and Adaptation

### Special Operations Command, Pacific, Assessment

When Fridovich replaced General Trebon as SOCPAC commander in January 2005, the ASG and JI had regrouped in and around the city of Jolo on the island of Jolo. Conditions on Basilan had improved during and after 2002 because of the advice and assistance the United States gave to the GRP. But ASG and JI operatives moved to Jolo and renewed their activities in and around the provincial capital of Jolo. The ASG and JI had exploited weak and long-neglected GRP governance and security structures and an impoverished local population that was sympathetic to their Islamist ideology. Many viewed Jolo City, Jolo's capital, as the "heart of darkness," a rugged island governed by a combination of radical Islam, myth, and violence. In addition, ASG and JI militants found the entire Sulu archipelago, of which Jolo was the capital, to be a hospitable environment indeed, permitting freedom of movement from island to island, as well as easy access to Malaysia.

Given these developments, Fridovich sought to redouble SOCPAC's earlier efforts to deny terrorists sanctuary in the southern Philippines. His first act was to order an assessment of the current conditions and effort in the area. On February 17, 2005, a SOCPAC and JSOTF-P team deployed to the Philippines to conduct a strategic-, operational-, and tactical-level assessment of OEF-P. The 2005 assessment, which concluded on March 11, used the TCAV assessment's findings and methodology to evaluate the current conditions. The SOCPAC assessment found significant problems on Jolo. Indicators showed that there were serious shortfalls in the local population's access to key essential services, including medical care, potable water, basic infrastructure, and education. However, the assessment also revealed key differences between the local culture in Jolo and that of Basilan.[1] History also loomed large: In the early 1900s, Jolo had been the site of heavy fighting between the U.S. Army and Muslim insurgents, and the locals had not forgotten. More recently, the MNLF, which had fought a bloody war against the AFP in the 1970s and incited periodic antigovernment violence ever since, also maintained a popular base on Jolo. AFP and JSOTF-P planners agreed that operations on Jolo could not succeed unless the MNLF remained on the sidelines and was com-

---

[1] The indigenous tribe of Sulu, the Tausug, had some distinct differences from the Yakan, the indigenous tribe of Basilan. The Tausug, or "people of the current," were a proud warrior culture, descended from seafaring people who had come from what is today Indonesia. In more-recent times, the Tausug had been implicated in banditry and piracy and had traded in their kris swords for rifles (interview 14, October 3, 2014; interview 63, December 6, 2014).

pelled to deny support to the ASG. Joint AFP/U.S. operations on Jolo could lead to intense, large-scale war if the MNLF reactivated its forces (interview 49, November 3, 2014; interview 61, October 31, 2014).

The assessment led Fridovich to deliver recommendations to USPACOM in March 2005 to increase operational assistance in the southern Philippines. His recommendations included expanding the advisory effort to focus on the Sulu archipelago and central Mindanao because the target threat groups had moved to these locations (interview 46, October 21, 2014). He recommended that the same population-centric approach used in Basilan be applied in Jolo. Intensive CMO in key areas could sway the population's sentiment in the Philippine government's favor and reduce the armed groups' freedom of movement. Although Jolo would be the focus of operations during this period, SOCPAC also recommended greater attention to the entire Sulu archipelago and central Mindanao.

The AFP had already surged troops into Jolo, but its combat-focused approach lacked intelligence and popular support. The Layas and Pugad operations of 2005 illustrated the shortcomings of this approach. The Philippine Marine Corps, which had assumed command of JTF Comet based on Jolo, sustained heavy casualties. U.S. SOF assisted with CASEVAC and emergency care provided by a U.S. FWD surgical team.

### Joint Special Operations Task Force—Philippines Moves South

The JSOTF-P commander, Colonel Linder, believed that his TF could help the AFP disrupt, degrade, and dismantle the terrorist networks that were operating on Jolo, which included not only the ASG and JI but also "rogue" MILF and MNLF elements. But Linder believed that, for this to work, JSOTF-P would need to change the way it operated so that it could focus more intensively on operations in the joint operations area (JOA).

Relocating to Zamboanga as JSOTF-P FWD was an important inflection point in OEF-P. It preceded some of the most intense and successful operations in OEF-P's history and put JSOTF-P on a new path of sustained operational assistance to AFP units throughout the JOA. Linder's rationale was simple: To have the desired effect on the fight, his TF needed to be closer to it, and its various elements needed to be better synchronized. So Linder moved JSOTF-P's HQ from the U.S. Embassy in Manila south to Mindanao, where he and his forces would establish a permanent FWD presence in Zamboanga at Camp Navarro. Linder left one JSOTF-P officer in the embassy as liaison and moved 23 to Zamboanga (interview 42, September 30, 2014). Linder himself spent approximately 75 percent of his time in the JOA (interview 61, October 31, 2014).

Linder decided to move JSOTF-P south both for practical and operational reasons. JSOTF-P had a limited number of forces, and its effectiveness was limited because available forces and capabilities were not organized in a way that optimized the commander's desired effects. In Linder's view, U.S. SOF deployed to JSOTF-P were of little use in Manila. They needed to be immersed in their operational environment down south in the JOA. JSOTF-P increased its manning, adding two ODAs in Jolo, one in Cotabato, and an NSW team in Davao in 2005 (interview 42, September 30, 2014). As JSOTF-P resumed its operational advisory assistance role and became widely distributed throughout the southern Philippines, the JSOTF-P manning grew steadily from 273 in 2005 to 607 in 2010.

### Preparation of the Environment

Following the SOCPAC assessment, JSOTF-P planners worked with the Philippine SOUTHCOM staff to develop a plan for deploying a TF to Jolo to replicate the success of the Basilan operations.[2] LTC Gregory Wilson and Philippine SOUTHCOM commander LTG Alberto Braganza met with Sulu province governor Benjamin Loong and other key local leaders to discuss plans to expand a U.S.-supported AFP effort in Jolo. Loong reportedly told the U.S. and AFP commanders, "I want on Sulu what you did on Basilan" (Colonel Wilson interview quoted in

[2] As with the Basilan TCAV assessment in late 2001, the pre-mission assessment and analysis gave JSOTF-P an advantage in planning operations that would be effective in Jolo localities that were ASG or JI strongholds.

Hastings and Mortela, 2008, p. 78).[3] Jolo leaders were invited to Camp Navarro to further discuss the terms and objectives of a U.S.-backed operation on Jolo.

CSM Frank Gilliand spent the last six weeks of his September 2005–February 2006 deployment to the Philippines preparing to move a company-sized element to Jolo. ODA 123 had established JTF Comet at Camp Bautista in October 2005. Gilliand's job was to set up its facilities. The team established a good relationship with the AFP Marine Corps, which gave U.S. SOF a large building for temporary use as a joint operations center, a dining hall, and living quarters (interview 42, September 30, 2014; interview 22, October 7, 2014). The lack of available electricity in Jolo was perhaps the most vexing infrastructure challenge in preparing for operating in Jolo. Eventually, a generator was shipped by boat, a 16-hour journey from Mindanao.

In September 2005, *bayanihan* ("community spirit") exercises began in Sulu; in February 2006, 250 U.S. troops arrived in Jolo as part of a larger Balikatan exercise. When the Balikatan exercise ended in early March, the U.S. forces in Jolo stayed on and conducted targeted CMO, including building deepwater wells, roads, and schools, and a series of medical civic action programs (MEDCAPs) and dental civic action programs to build goodwill with the population in ASG areas (interview 49, November 3, 2014; interview 14, October 3, 2014; interview 61, October 31, 2014). Initially, JSOTF-P focused capacity-building efforts on fixed-site security and convoy escort to enable development efforts. In short, U.S. forces began implementing JSOTF-P command Colonel Linder's strategy of "surrounding the enemy with goodness" (interview 49, November 3, 2014). Simultaneously, JSOTF-P and the AFP increased information gathering and intelligence efforts to develop a clear enemy situation, and the NSW component of JSOTF-P began training maritime units to increase their capabilities, to interact with local fishers to gather information, and to interdict smuggling

[3] According to Wilson, several of the local Sulu leaders voiced concern that the United States' real interest in Jolo was to search for and steal Japanese gold, which, according to urban legend, was located on the island or just offshore. This was also a common ASG propaganda theme during AFP and U.S. operations on Jolo (see Hastings and Mortela, 2008, p. 78).

activity to deny insurgents' resources (interview 49, November 3, 2014; interview 34, October 10, 2014).

Pre-mission assessments suggested that Ultimatum's complex requirements and the AFP's lead combat role would require JSOTF-P to build AFP capacity that would translate into the necessary AFP elements possessing the specific capabilities required for the operation under JSOTF-P's plans for the operation, which JSOTF-P operations directorate (J-3) MAJ Scott Malone had designed.[4]

## Operation Ultimatum: Plan Execution

JSOTF-P's principal partner for operations on Jolo and the fight against the ASG and JI was JTF Comet, which consisted of an Army BDE, two Marine Corps BDEs, a joint SOF, the 9th Tactical Operations Group (Air), and Naval TG 61. In addition, JSOTF-P supported AFP commands in Mindanao.

The JSOTF-P received a significant increase in joint and interagency personnel and capabilities during this period, in particular naval and air assets that amplified the task force's geographic reach in a maritime environment. As such, the small JSOTF-P mission was well equipped to provide support to various AFP CT efforts, providing expertise and capabilities that were beyond what the U.S. SOF could have mustered on its own.

Operation Ultimatum began August 1, 2006, and concluded in October 2007. This operation, or, more accurately, series of operations, aimed to take down the ASG's network in Jolo. In the process, a fundamental change occurred in how the AFP conducted its operations. In addition to new competence in planning and conducting large-scale combat operations, the AFP embraced CMO as a major element of its campaign. "CMO are not as sexy as combat operations, but I told

[4] Malone's role as the key architect of Operation Ultimatum was noted by Major General Linder, who assumed command of JSOTF-P after Malone had already begun planning Ultimatum. Linder remained commander through Ultimatum's initial phase until Colonel Maxwell assumed command of JSOTF-P for the remainder of the Ultimatum operations (interview 49, November 3, 2014; interview 45, October 16, 2014).

my marines that CMO is saving soldiers' lives," one Philippine general stated. "I required all my marines to go through a seminar on Islam and the Tausug traditions. . . . The problem in the south is that we have been treating the Muslims there as second-class citizens" (interview 22, October 7, 2014). Figure 4.1 illustrates the operation.

In the months prior to the initiation of Operation Ultimatum on August 1, 2006, JSOTF-P and AFP elements began training in order to build capacity to conduct offensive operations as part of Operation Ultimatum. Beginning in April, JSOTF-P and their AFP counterparts conducted rehearsals, planning, and intelligence activities and continued to engage in CMO in order to ensure favorable conditions for Ultimatum. The pre-Ultimatum preparation of the environment was

**Figure 4.1**
**Diagram of Operation Ultimatum Concept**

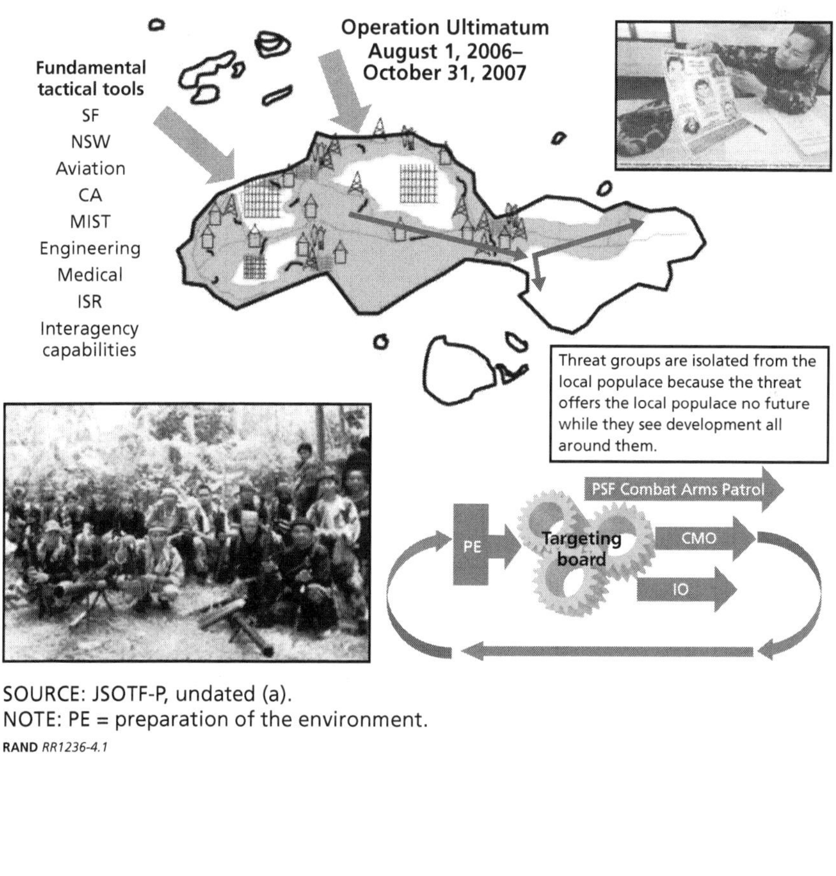


SOURCE: JSOTF-P, undated (a).
NOTE: PE = preparation of the environment.
RAND *RR1236-4.1*

unprecedented, even in comparison with the 2001–2002 Basilan operations. The AFP had never before conducted or participated in such large-scale, joint combined rehearsals. Extensive maritime interdiction operations were also conducted. The planning, rehearsals, and combined employment of U.S. and AFP resources would prove to be key to Operation Ultimatum's success.

JSOTF-P and AFP planners had identified four initial objectives: Tubora Hill, Camp Timahu, Mount Kagay, and Mount Taran. On July 29, AFP forces began moving into position, slowly increasing their presence in the objective areas in order to provide support to the main effort. Securing these objectives would provide a GRP foothold into key ASG and JI areas and help to deny militants support from the Indanan population, which planners expected to cause the militants to flee. By isolating Indanan both on land and at sea, militants who attempted to flee would be trapped by the strategically placed blocking forces.

Shortly after midnight on August 1, 2006, AFP joint forces conducted an amphibious landing that was synchronized with prepositioned ground forces. Almost 300 AFP sailors, marines, and soldiers crossed the beach to pursue their objectives. Marine, LRC and NAVSOG elements simultaneously executed blocking and deception operations. These initial operations were followed by efforts to surround the ASG and flush them from the MNLF camps where leaders were hiding. AFP marines and soldiers from the 35th Infantry Brigade applied enormous pressure to the insurgent positions on Tubora Hill and Mount Kagay in the north while LRC operators closed in on high-value target positions at Camp Timahu in the west. The amphibious assault coupled with the advancing infantry attack in the south and on the western slope of Mount Tumatangis gave the insurgents nowhere to run. Insurgent forces quickly splintered into small elements and spent the majority of the first day bouncing into one AFP unit after another while taking heavy casualties, including Ismin Sahiron, the son of ASG senior leader Radullan Sahiron.

AFP units secured their initial objectives by noon on the first day of Operation Ultimatum, established security positions, and prepared for pursuit operations as follow-on to their initial successes. The AFP had taken the insurgents by complete surprise, removing them from a safe haven they had enjoyed for more than 30 years.

JSOTF-P assisted in coordinating the operation's complex deception and targeting elements through LCEs stationed at BN command posts and higher-level HQ. The LCEs' all-source intelligence and communication equipment provided situational awareness both to the Filipinos and the other American advisers, and JSOTF-P was standing by to provide CASEVAC to wounded AFP troops.

#### *Tactical-Level Advise and Assist*

The ROE had been revised in the most recent guidance issued by USPACOM, which allowed JSOTF-P troops to be in a combat environment provided that they positioned themselves in locations where they would not come into contact with the enemy. The previous guidance had permitted battalion-level advising, which meant that JSOTF-P LCEs could accompany AFP battalion-level command staff as they established forward command posts. This was the case on Jolo during Operation Ultimatum.

CPT Herb Daniels led a split team assigned to advise the 51st BN, which was new to combat operations and inexperienced in jungle terrain. In the weeks prior to Operation Ultimatum, the team focused on improving the unit's soldier- and unit-level skills and hardening the base's fortifications. The battalion had already instituted formal courses for its NCOs, which the SOF team took as a heartening sign of AFP professionalization; U.S. forces rely heavily on NCOs for tactical-level leadership. The team also conducted assessments and CMO in the Talipao municipality. Although U.S. SOF were prohibited from engaging in combat patrols, U.S. forces were permitted to patrol 4 km around their base after dark. Initial patrols brought enemy fire, but, after a few weeks of patrolling, the unit was no longer taking fire. The activity pushed the ASG out or into a quiescent posture. The joint patrols also raised the confidence level of the 51st BN (interview 14, October 3, 2014).

When Operation Ultimatum began on August 1, the 51st received a warning order to push north in the next 48 hours. The unit moved from its mountain base to western Jolo, where the ASG had been coming in and out of an MNLF base camp. Daniels's split team was the only one authorized to leave base camp with its AFP counterpart unit, which made them Colonel Linder's only JSOTF-P eyes and ears on the battlefield.

AFP units planned to push the ASG down from the north toward blocking positions to the southwest below Mount Tumatangis formed by two of Daniels's counterpart AFP companies, which the LCE supported with ISR from P-3 aircraft. These elements moved into place under cover of night with no hostile engagements. But eventually, these positions were surrounded. Daniels advised moving the command post to Mount Teran, which was a 12-hour march through the jungle. The element maneuvered to Mount Teran, overrunning an ASG camp of young recruits in the process. The operation was not planned to last more than ten days, but the post remained at Mount Teran amid intense combat for more than three weeks without resupply. Daniels's team was extracted after the prolonged engagement. The vignette illustrates how U.S. forces were, at times, able to advise and assist at the tactical level during combat operations.

### *The Abu Solaiman Operation*

The death of ASG leader Abu Solaiman (an alias; his real name was Jainal Antel Sali, Jr.) marked not only the significant degradation of ASG leadership but also the adoption of numerous operational approaches that JSOTF-P had been seeking to impart to its partners. The development of a supportive population, intelligence collection, and the implementation of a law enforcement–based plan to capture him were all new elements of the AFP approach to CT. In March 2006, the ASG bombed a food co-op in Jolo City that resulted in the deaths of five Muslim citizens. At least 20 others were wounded in the incident. The ASG attack on the co-op and the civilian casualties inflicted against members of the Muslim local population ended up being helpful: The AFP used it to drive a wedge between the ASG and the population and used population support to enable effective targeting. The response came from within the ASG and from without. Internally, ASG members questioned whether their operations should harm Muslim civilians. The wife of one mid-level ASG member disapproved of her husband's activities and membership in the group and complained that the ASG was not even feeding their family. She was instrumental in convincing her husband to turn against the ASG, at least partly to claim the $5 million reward for information leading to the capture or killing of Abu Solaiman as part of the United States' Rewards for Justice program. According to the JSOTF-P commander at the time, the woman brought her husband leaflets touting a reward for Abu Solaiman, which had been produced jointly by U.S. and Philippine PSYOP teams expressly for this purpose (interview 68, November 4, 2014; interview 45, October 16, 2014).

The ASG member was "turned" as a clandestine informant by a Philippine intelligence unit, which developed the source throughout spring 2006 and early winter 2007. In early 2007, the source obtained and shared Abu Solaiman's cell phone number. JSOTF-P had requested and received additional U.S. intelligence support to be provided to its HQ, which was instrumental in assisting with the Philippine operation while observing U.S. intelligence protocols (interview 45, October 16, 2014; interview 38, October 11, 2014). In January 2007, Abu Solaiman's precise location was identified on Jolo, and the information was transmitted to the U.S. SF ODA advising the AFP 8th SF company on the island. Despite difficult terrain and weather conditions, the SF company conducted a ground infiltration through some of Jolo's highest mountains and assaulted Abu Solaiman's camp at first light. During a 75-minute firefight, Abu Solaiman was killed, as were two AFP soldiers (JSOTF-P, 2008a, slide 27).

The Abu Solaiman operation succeeded because of effective fusion of intelligence and operations and efforts by law enforcement and the U.S. State Department that yielded the critical intelligence on Abu Solaiman's location. Abu Solaiman, also known as "the Engineer," had been indicted in U.S. court in 2002 on charges of involvement in terrorist acts, which included hostage kidnapping and murder against U.S. nationals and other foreign nationals in and around the GRP. In 2006, the Federal Bureau of Investigation added Abu Solaiman to its Most Wanted Terrorists list, along with two other members of the ASG. Under the U.S. government's Rewards for Justice program, a $5 million reward was offered for information leading to his capture.

Operations against Abu Solaiman and other ASG leaders marked significant operational successes aided by law enforcement. Two $5 million payouts were made through the Rewards for Justice program, one for information leading to the death of Abu Solaiman and the other for information leading to the death of Janjalani, whom the AFP had killed in August 2006. This program became more successful after the JSOTF-P PSYOP team worked with State Department counterparts on the U.S. country team to effectively combine the DoD and Department of State Rewards for Justice programs, greatly incentivizing information-sharing by local nationals in JSOTF-P's JOA (interview 68, November 4, 2014).

### Joint Special Operations Task Force—Philippines Continuity of Approach and Interagency Cooperation

Maxwell returned to the Philippines as commander of JSOTF-P in mid-2007 while Operation Ultimatum was under way. Maxwell was a career SF officer, while Linder had spent his career in classified SOF units, but both realized that, in the environment in which they were operating as commanders of JSOTF-P, the Basilan model was necessary to achieve the objectives laid out in JSOTF-P's mission statement. While he continued the same basic approach set by the SOCPAC assessment and recommendations, Maxwell made several adjustments of emphasis in his mission statement, lines of operation, and locus of activity. He reemphasized population-centric aspects of the strategy.

In addition, the movement of key terrorist leaders back to Basilan led Maxwell to put an ODA back on the island in September 2007, while retaining the focus on Jolo and central Mindanao. He also oversaw the creation of TF Archipelago, which NSW would command, as a subordinate TF to oversee all operations on Basilan and the entire Sulu archipelago down to Tawi-Tawi, where an NSW element would remain for the next six years.

Maxwell's mission statement reemphasized the building of PSF capacity as the vehicle for successful CT operations. It read,

> In coordination with the country team, [JSOTF-P] builds capacity and strengthens the Republic of the Philippines' security

> forces to defeat selected terrorist organizations in order to protect US and Filipino citizens and interests from terrorist attack while preserving Philippine sovereignty. (Maxwell, undated [b])

Specifically, Maxwell directed his troops to enable AFP to execute four main tasks:

1. Deny insurgent and terrorist sanctuary.
2. Deny insurgent and terrorist mobility.
3. Deny insurgent and terrorist access to resources.
4. Separate the population from the insurgent and terrorist.

Each of these four counterinsurgency tasks was consistent with methods that were being touted back in Washington, both in the new Army/Marine Corps' *Counterinsurgency* Field Manual (FM) 3-24 (HQ, Department of the Army, 2006) and among the national security intellectual community inside and outside the government. However, the critical difference in the Philippines was that Philippine forces were leading and conducting these operations, while U.S. troops were doing so in Iraq and Afghanistan. Under the OEF-P ROE, U.S. troops could not directly engage in combat operations, but they could train, advise, and assist the host-nation forces in doing so. The JSOTF-P did so through four lines of operation:

1. capacity-building of PSF
2. targeted CMO
3. intelligence operations
4. IO.

These four lines of operation continued, with some variation in emphasis and wording, throughout the OEF-P campaign. Thus, despite the turnover in commanders and JSOTF-P staff, a fair degree of continuity of effort was maintained.

Per Maxwell's end-of-tour report, the JSOTF-P consisted of a 66-person HQ with various detached elements totaling about 500 personnel. Most of JSOTF-P's personnel rotated every six months. However, three key positions were one-year tours: commander, command sergeant major, and the J-3 operations officer. Numerous interviewees stated that the longer tours were critical to achieve sustained operational effects with the AFP partners, as well as influence within the U.S. country team in Manila. According to one interviewee,

> You can't make any impact with State if you aren't going to be in country for at least a year. So we made a concerted effort to keep people in country longer so that they'd be integrated more closely with the team.

Maxwell, who, as JSOTF-P commander, had engaged closely with the U.S. embassy, wrote the following in his end-of-tour report:

> One of the most unique aspects of this mission is the synchronization of JSOTF operations with the US Country Team. There is an extremely close working relationship with most elements of the country team and in particular USAID. The Country Team conducts numerous activities that directly support operations in the Joint Operational Area in the Southern Philippines, to include the Rewards for Justice, USAID sustainable development projects, 1206/1207 Funding, Intelligence support from the entire intelligence community as well as from [the legal attaché, or LEGAT], Treasury, and other elements. The JSOTF maintains permanent liaison with the Country Team and the command group participates in weekly country team meetings and has a standing weekly brief to the Ambassador. (Maxwell, undated [a])[5]

Kristie A. Kenney proved to be a very hands-on ambassador who phoned JSOTF-P several times a week, in addition to Maxwell's weekly visits to Manila to brief her and attend embassy meetings. The ambassador required that all press and public information activities be coordinated and receive embassy approval; the previous commander had not always followed this practice (interview 64, December 4, 2014).

---

5 The phrase *1206/1207 funding* refers to two sections, 1206 and 1207, of the National Defense Authorization Act (NDAA) for Fiscal Year (FY) 2006, Public Law 109-163, 2006, which provide, respectively, authority to build the capacity of foreign military forces and security and stabilization assistance.

The U.S. embassy actively supported the renewed U.S. activity in the southern Philippines. Both Ambassador Ricciardone and Ambassador Kenney visited several times, usually with a senior Philippine official. Numerous key GRP ministers visited development projects and pledged support to local government officials, marking a new activism and interest on the part of the Manila government. In addition, the U.S. embassy sought to ensure that U.S. military activities did not negatively affect the GRP's effort to reach negotiated settlements with the Moro separatists. Finally, both ambassadors ensured an open flow of information and briefings to GRP officials, reinforcing the message that the U.S. military effort respected the prerogatives and priorities of the Philippine government. Renewed terms of reference were established in the Kapit Bisig agreement signed in July 2006 between USPACOM and the AFP. It reiterated the previous terms that U.S. activities would be approved by the GRP, would not include combat outside of legitimate self-defense, and would not entail establishment of permanent U.S. bases or support facilities.

## Summary

During 2005–2007, U.S. SOF conducted an assessment-driven adaptation of the plan and expanded its efforts based on a newly active transnational threat in the Sulu archipelago and central Mindanao. JSOTF-P HQ moved from Manila to Mindanao and increased its footprint to conduct wider operational advising and assistance activities. Subordinate TF Mindanao was expanded, and TF Archipelago was established to oversee U.S. operations on Basilan and throughout the Sulu archipelago; new LCEs were established and ISR platforms increased.

JSOTF-P applied the Basilan model to Jolo Island, conducting extensive CMO in advance of and in conjunction with large-scale joint and maritime combat operations by the Philippine armed forces. Operational advice and enabling support were provided throughout. The extended campaign, known as Operation Ultimatum, also relied extensively on MISO programs, including the combined DoD/Department of State Rewards for Justice program to introduce a substantially new law enforcement element to the overall approach to defeating transnational terrorist groups in the Philippines.

The principal outcomes of this period were the degradation of the threat on Jolo, increased Philippine military capability in joint operations, Philippine military embrace of CMO, and increased involvement by Manila government officials and ministries in the southern Philippines. U.S. SOF contributed to each of these outcomes substantially.

The Philippine armed forces, with support from JSOTF-P, delivered decisive blows to the ASG leadership on Jolo, including the confirmed deaths of key leaders Abu Solaiman and Khadaffy Janjalani. Enemy-initiated attacks fell by almost 50 percent from their 2001 levels (ESOC, undated). On Basilan, during the period 2005–2007, enemy-initiated attacks fell from 28 in 2005 to ten in 2007. Only six enemy-initiated attacks occurred in 2006. In Sulu province, the enemy's main effort during this period, enemy-initiated attacks dropped from 56 in 2005 to 43 in 2006 and 31 in 2007—a 57.5-percent decrease (see Figure 4.2). Attacks remained low on Tawi-Tawi during this period.

The ASG proved unable to amass forces or conduct sustained operations on Jolo, leading some to conclude that the back of the ASG as a terrorist organization had been definitively broken.

The Philippine military, with U.S. advice and enablers, developed significant capability in executing complex joint operations, as well as robust use of CMO, to achieve objectives, and these operations led to decreased freedom of movement and popular support for the ASG. The population of Jolo responded to U.S. and Philippine CMO and IO with support for military operations and information that directly supported mission objectives, including the capture of ASG leadership. Through visits and increased funding, the national government expanded efforts to meet economic and political needs of the population in the southern Philippines. Both the U.S. embassy and JSOTF-P provided concrete support to these efforts, accompanying the visits and underwriting assistance programs.

**Figure 4.2**
**Enemy-Initiated Incidents in Basilan, Sulu, and Tawi-Tawi, 2005–2007**

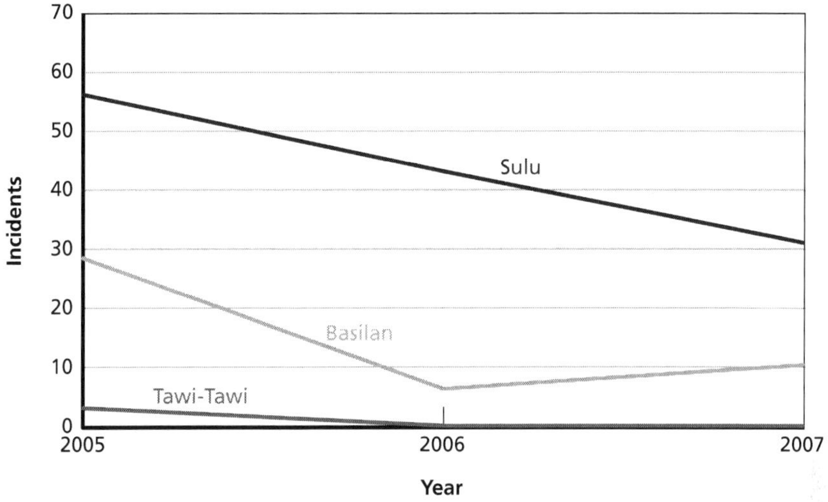


SOURCE: ESOC data.
NOTE: Incidents are counts of enemy-initiated incidents per year by province.
RAND RR1236-4.2

CHAPTER FIVE

# 2008–2010: Expansion of Effort

2008 brought a new crisis to the southern Philippines, as the government's talks with the MNLF broke down. A major offensive ensued in central Mindanao, which included marshy and mountainous terrain where many of the threat groups found refuge. In addition, AFP marines were beheaded in Basilan in a grisly attack. The successful operations on Jolo gave way to a renewed focus by JSOTF-P on Basilan and central Mindanao. In addition to the widest geographic expansion of OEF-P, JSOTF-P undertook several initiatives to build new AFP capabilities that it hoped would achieve decisive effects in the long-running conflict.

In July 2007, a convoy of Philippine marines on a mission to find Italian priest Giancarlo Bossi, who had been kidnapped in Zamboanga Sibugay province, was ambushed in Al-Barka municipality in southeast Basilan, where Bossi was reportedly being held. In all, 14 marines were killed in the incident; ten of the bodies were beheaded. The MILF claimed that the marines were trespassing on their land. More than 100 suspects, including ASG and MILF members, were charged with the murder of the Philippine marines (International Crisis Group, 2012, p. 8).

In response to these events, the AFP deployed additional forces to Basilan. The response to the attack and beheadings of the marines, according to a commander who was in the Philippines both in 2002 and in 2007, was "like night and day"; the AFP and the Philippine marines in particular had been known for heavy-handed tactics, and their response to the 2007 incident displayed a new, more-restrained, more-sophisticated approach to the use of force (interview 45, October 16, 2014). They deployed more SOF to Basilan, along with additional engineers and medical personnel, to bolster the CMO-targeting method that had been successful previously on Basilan and Sulu. This approach contrasted with the indiscriminate fires that marked many AFP responses before and during the initial phase of OEF-P (interview 66, November 7, 2014; interview 45, October 16, 2014).

Meanwhile, violence continued around the region during the summer, including a string of bus bombings in Mindanao that killed at least 19 and injured dozens (International Crisis Group, 2008, p. 8). In November, former Basilan governor Wahab M. Akbar, a former ASG leader who had turned supportive of the U.S. and GRP efforts, was killed in a bombing outside the House of Representatives in Manila, where he served as a legislator.

Central Mindanao become the scene of major fighting in 2008 as the peace talks with the MILF broke down; hundreds were killed and tens of thousands displaced. JSOTF-P increased its role in Mindanao because the ASG and JI were operating in the area, nested within the other armed groups. TF Mindanao conducted a wide variety of training, advising, and assistance activities in addition to intelligence, MEDEVAC, CMO, and IO with new units of the AFP.

## Assessment and Adaptation

In 2008, USPACOM conducted an assessment of OEF-P, which concluded that the principal objectives had been met (i.e., the ASG threat was degraded) and that planning for transition could begin. This assessment was not acted upon for several reasons. Several events created new turmoil in the southern Philippines, including increased activity by the ASG in Basilan, the breakdown of GRP–MNLF talks, and an offensive in central Mindanao. Under the new JSOTF-P commander, COL William Coultrup, new activities were undertaken that refocused the effort. The embassy supported efforts to target key remaining leaders of the ASG and JI as an important step toward successful transition.

Colonel Coultrup had been notified of his assignment to JSOTF-P while finishing war college; the Army selected promotable colonels to fill the position, often with little notice. Maxwell had been willing to stay on, but U.S. Army Special Operations Command ordered him to report to duty as the chief of operations at the Fort Bragg command. As it turned out, Coultrup, who had served in a special mission unit, would become the longest-serving JSOTF-P commander, for three years: from 2008 to 2010.

As Coultrup developed an in-depth appreciation for the distinct differences of each island, he fashioned a decentralized approach to accommodate those differences (interview 63, December 6, 2014). What worked in Basilan, for example, would not necessarily work in Jolo or in central Mindanao. He tasked his subordinate commanders to develop and implement solutions appropriate for their AORs in coordination with AFP partners, as well as the GRP and U.S. embassy. JSOTF-P committed more than $24 million to humanitarian assistance projects between late 2007 and mid-2011; between 2008 and 2012, USAID was slated to spend $98.9 million through its GEM 3 program.

Coultrup also spearheaded a renewed effort to help the AFP develop a precision-targeting capability, based on his assessment and that of Philippine commanders that the AFP lacked this ability to fix and finish targets. Third, he undertook more-robust IO, which included outreach to local and international media. USPACOM assigned a public affairs officer to JSOTF-P, who issued more-frequent press releases, and a blog was launched for the command. These efforts, as well as media outreach by previous commanders, had caused some friction with the embassy, which not only wanted to vet all public messages but also believed very strongly that the Philippine government should be the central source and object of attention, rather than the U.S. forces. Although they did not disagree with the principle of host-nation lead, some JSOTF-P members believed that IO could be more robust and effective.

## Plan Execution

### Decentralized Operations

The restiveness on Basilan and elsewhere led the United States to expand its effort from its previous focus on Jolo, and Sulu province more broadly, during Operation Ultimatum. Three subordinate TFs were set up to adopt tailored approaches to the distinct problems of each area: TF Mindanao, TF Sulu, and TF Archipelago. See Figure 5.1 for the disposition of forces.

The array of armed groups in the southern Philippines had always complicated U.S. operations because the terms of reference for OEF-P prohibited the United States from supporting operations against the MNLF and MILF, with which the GRP was engaged in a peace process. Yet relationships among the ASG, the JI, and other Islamist groups in the ARMM, such as the MILF and the MNLF, enabled the ASG to find sanctuary, recruits, and assistance in areas they controlled. The MNLF, for example, had roughly 3,000 irregular combatants who

**Figure 5.1**
**Disposition of Forces as of September 2007**

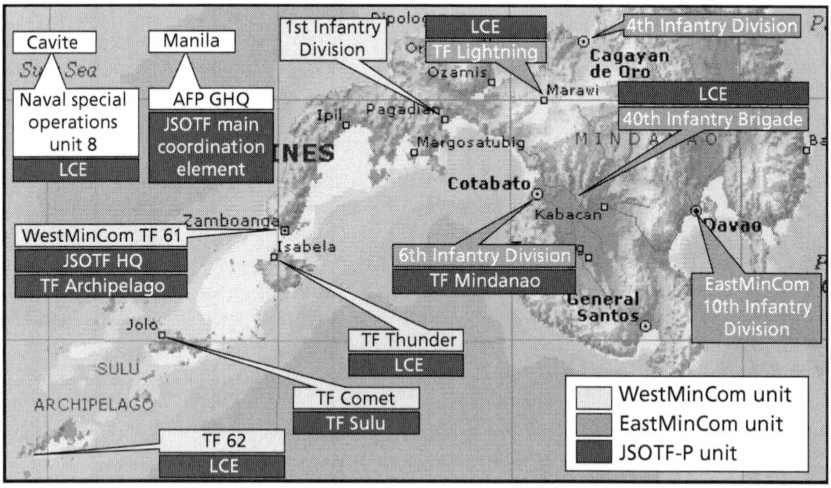


SOURCE: JSOTF-P, 2007b.
NOTE: GHQ = general HQ.
RAND *RR1236-5.1*

never had to disarm or integrate with the AFP following the MNLF's 1996 peace accord with the GRP. One "rogue" MNLF unit, frustrated with the government's failure to implement the accord, renewed hostilities in 2007, and MNLF cadres gave active or tacit support to the ASG, with which they are tied by blood or clan (Abuza, 2012, p. 6).

This aspect of intermingled and co-dependent threat groups was never fully dealt with. Some U.S. SOF officers believed that a combined campaign should have been developed to address these linkages more systematically (International Crisis Group, 2008, p. 21; see also Wilson, 2006, p. 9). Some of the JSOTF-P personnel interviewed referred to the rank-and-file fighters as "shirt changers." Yet, so long as the government policy was to engage the MNLF and then the MILF in peace talks leading to an eventual negotiated settlement, the option of outright combat against all the armed groups did not exist.

Coultrup decentralized nonkinetic operations to enable the teams to determine where and what types of activities were needed. Previously, the JSOTF-P commander had had a centralized target board in the Zamboanga HQ. One commander noted that initiating any JSOTF-P project required permission and support from the local Philippine CA units, the AFP, and the Filipino civilian leadership. With regard to the last, local Filipino politicians frequently leveraged JSOTF-P projects to enhance their reelection campaigns.

### *Task Force Sulu*

Jolo continued to be a sanctuary for armed groups. Politicians were adept at manipulating violence to ensure that resources flowed into the area. Interviewees suggested that Sulu governor Abdusakur Mahail Tan knew he could not expect the central government to give him resources. The ARMM headquarters, located in central Mindanao, did not prioritize the Sulu archipelago, and money intended for development rarely reached his island. Consequently, to get aid money and attention from the GRP and the U.S. government, Tan and local politicians allowed the ASG to engage in infractions with the expectation that they would receive resources that they could exploit for political reasons, such as local projects conducted during CMO, which the United States funded but for which the AFP was usually given credit for conducting. Targeting the ASG in Jolo, where it had protection and support from the governor, required JSOTF-P to put pressure on the governor. If Tan was supportive in efforts to pursue the ASG, JSOTF-P would encourage the embassy to provide more resources from USAID and other programs. With such aid, the Sulu archipelago could develop its coffee industry, tourism, and other business. If Tan continued to collaborate with local ASG elements, the country team might threaten to cut off such aid (interview 63, December 6, 2014).

#### *Task Force Mindanao*

TF Mindanao was located in Cotabato, in central Mindanao, where its primary AFP partner was the 6th Infantry Division (interview 61, October 31, 2014). Initially, an additional ODA was sent to Cotabato along with intelligence assets, and an SF company was split between TF Sulu and TF Mindanao. In 2009 and 2010, JSOTF-P expanded to include a BN command in Cotabato, with company commands on Mindanao, Basilan, and Jolo. The JSOTF also sent additional manpower to assist the Navy SEALs on Basilan.

At TF Mindanao, a SOTF BN conducted expanded advise-and-assist operations, as well as capacity-building efforts, with the AFP's 6th Infantry Division. The 6th Infantry Division was not a very well-trained or -equipped partner force. TF Mindanao found that the 6th Infantry Division BNs and companies struggled with basic combat patrol, maneuver, and artillery functions. They therefore decided to focus on basic training and fundamental skills. According to officers who worked with this unit over time, the 6th Infantry Division became competent in basic tactical skills and capable of conducting effective operations in its AOR (interview 4, October 2, 2014; interview 37, October 10, 2014; interview 36, October 10, 2014).

JSOTF-P's command and staff officers continued their predecessors' practice of devoting most of their time to WestMinCom, the command in Zamboanga. However, the J-2 and J-3 added a weekly visit to EastMinCom areas to demonstrate JSOTF-P's interest in all partner efforts, not just those in WestMinCom's AOR.

In Cotabato, the AFP's main target was Abdul Basit Usman, a MILF commander who provided support and safe haven to the ASG and the JI. The U.S. TF increased its activities in central Mindanao because JI safe-haven areas effectively separated the AFP and Philippine National Police (PNP) from the population in the mountains and marsh areas, leaving it under the control of the JI and other Islamist elements (interview 63, December 6, 2014). CA teams were very active in central Mindanao. CA teams supported a USAID Arms to Farms program, in which MILF and MNLF fighters gave up their weapons in exchange for plots of land. JSOTF-P CA teams assisted their Filipino counterparts in running this program. Disagreements sometimes occurred over where and how to implement the program. In one case, USAID and JSOTF-P leadership disagreed over the type of fish to be used in a fish-farming initiative, so the latter funded the program.

### *Task Force Archipelago*

From mid-2008 through 2010, the main problem on Basilan was weak governance. Akbar's departure for Manila had left a power vacuum in Basilan, which his three wives attempted to fill. One wife was a Christian, and the other two were Muslim. But tribalism was as important as religion, and tribal leaders working with the ASG were more powerful than the shaky arrangement that Akbar had left behind, which deteriorated further after his death.

U.S. NSW led TF Archipelago, which oversaw TF operations on Basilan and Tawi-Tawi, as well as the maritime area, and SEALs assigned to advise the NAVSOG HQ. The size of the NSW presence fluctuated over time, from a low of 15 in 2006 to a high of 55 in 2008 (interview 74, November 5, 2014).

In 2006, NSW focused on Jolo, advising the Philippine Naval Task Force on where to place its ships to stop the ASG from moving between islands. NSW elements also helped to advise, assist, and transport NAVSOG elements and trained them on tactical operations (interview 34, October 9, 2014). One interviewee judged that the maritime interdiction operations during Operation Ultimatum had limited impact in either mapping the facilitation network or in dismantling it; another interviewee stated that his NSW forces "burned a hole around Jolo for six months." Philippine naval units would accept bribes or money to transport or siphon off fuel or goods. NSW strove to inculcate professional behavior and persuade its counterparts of the operational benefits of working with the population in the area (interview 49, November 3, 2014).

By 2010, TF Archipelago consisted of 14 SEALs and a total of 130 personnel, including U.S. Marine Corps force reconnaissance, U.S. Army Green Berets, logisticians, and a boat detachment that had two Mark Vs, four rigid-hulled inflatable boats, and maritime support vessels. Forward operating bases were established in Basilan, Tawi-Tawi, and remote islands, with the HQ in Zamboanga (interview 48, November 6, 2014). In 2011, TF Archipelago increased in size to a full SEAL platoon (PLT) (about 20), a Marine Corps special operations team (MSOT), MIST, and CA teams. TF Archipelago worked with more than just AFP naval elements; on Basilan, it advised and assisted conventional Philippine Army, Philippine SF Regiment (SFR), and Scout Ranger Regiment (SRR) units. They also conducted CMO and met frequently with the local government units (interview 70, December 3, 2014). One AFP commander praised the NSW work and arranged a medal for one of the NSW members who rescued AFP troops under fire; he also appreciated the occasional transport provided by NSW (interview 36; October 10, 2014).

The NSW Mark V and rigid-hulled inflatable boats provided an extremely useful capability to transport both U.S. and Philippine forces, as well as to train Philippine naval and NAVSOG units in boat tactics and maintenance. In the early years, either the Philippine elements did not have the boats or the boats they had were old and poorly maintained. TF Archipelago also provided ISR and medical support. The MSOTs provided a great deal of medical assistance, and, during operations, they would feed the Philippine elements intelligence from ISR. TF Archipelago was supported by an NSW ScanEagle detachment for a time, until a contracted element replaced it. Technicians extended the UAV range of coverage through a hub-and-spoke system. TF Archipelago aided joint planning and operations among the AFP services and, in particular, tried to foster cooperation between Philippine SEALs and SFR and SRR elements, beginning with persuading NAVSOG to use its craft to transport the rangers and SF for operations.

## Increased Emphasis on Armed Forces of Philippines Targeting of Abu Sayyaf Group Leaders

Coultrup shifted JSOTF-P's focus to improve the AFP's ability to target ASG leaders. He encountered several obstacles, including a lack of will on the part of some Philippine commanders and key local officials, as well as gaps in AFP capability to prosecute targets. Whereas the AFP had eagerly embraced the CMO, they were still not achieving consistent effects desired on the kinetic side. According to a former commander,

> The nonkinetic side [of getting approval to conduct these operations] was relatively easy, but on [the] kinetic side was much more difficult. I could come up with the best target package, but convincing them to go in was sometimes a huge challenge, as far as convincing them to do it. (interview 63, December 6, 2014)

Although political will remained a problem, the one obstacle Coultrup could affect was a lack of military capability to fix and finish targets with a minimum of collateral damage.

The AFP capability to find targets was fairly well developed, primarily because of its excellent HUMINT networks. However, the AFP was unable to fix and finish targets because it lacked precision munitions and the means to deliver them. Numerous interviewees described the continued use of tactics, such as launching massive barrages of artillery fire in the general direction of massed enemy forces, with limited ability to avoid civilian casualties, and dumb bombs dropped from planes that often, because of the age of the ordnance, failed to detonate. The AFP understood the negative effects of indiscriminate fires, but they lacked the proper equipment and training to deliver more-precise firepower. Many munitions and platforms were old and sometimes barely functional.

JSOTF-P sought to improve the AFP's strike capabilities by various means. The first initiative enabled the PAF to transition from dumb bombs to fuzed bombs delivered by its OV-10 planes. The initial requests seeking to fund this program through Section 1208 authorities did not meet the needed criteria (aiding indigenous forces that were conducting CT operations alongside U.S. forces).[1] Coultrup then sought and found alternative funding for training and equipment for OV-10s to transition to fuzed bombs, which were successfully used in operations.

Next, Coultrup sought to improve AFP strike capabilities via precision-guided artillery. He arranged for Marine Corps howitzers to be temporarily emplaced on Jolo and Philippine forces to be supplied with precision-guided artillery rounds. This technique was only partially successful because of inadequate training and employment of the artillery. Coultrup's next initiative aimed to put "smart" bombs on "dumb" PAF aircraft. He devoted a great deal of his time investigating the technical requirements, preparing and shepherding a request for such assistance through the U.S. security assistance channels. Almost two years after he began his efforts, the program was funded in the FY 2010 budget through Section 1206 funding authorities.[2] Training and equipping began shortly before his departure.

### Intelligence, Surveillance, and Reconnaissance Platforms and Intelligence Support

At the same time, as part of JSOTF-P's increased focus on supporting kinetic targeting, the number and types of ISR platforms increased and provided greater collection capacity and support for AFP and PNP operations. The main ISR platform that was used during the early period of OEF-P was the P-3 aircraft, which was described as providing IMINT of limited value. Suited for submarine hunting, it was less optimal for tracking small groups in triple-canopy jungle. Over time, the TF obtained additional ISR assets, from tactical UAVs to manned

---

[1] Section 1208 is another relevant section of the NDAA for FY 2006; it provides for reimbursement of certain coalition nations for support that they provide to U.S. military operations.

[2] Serafino, 2013, p. 23, states,

> FY2010 assistance for the Philippines provided a precision guided missile capability to assist Philippine armed forces' CT efforts in southern regions to combat the activities of the Jimaah Islamijah and Abu Sayyuf Group ($18.4million), and weapons and equipment to build the Philippines' Marine Corps Force Reconnaissance Battalion's CT capacity ($9.3 million).

platforms that provided a great range of electro-optical, infrared, full-motion video, and SIGINT-collection capabilities.

Figure 5.2, from a February 2008 JSOTF-P briefing, shows the resources to which the JTF had access at the time.

The unmanned platform to which JSOTF-P had access for much of the campaign was the ScanEagle. It provided a lower-altitude, higher-resolution product from a platform with a long loiter time and, after modifications, a wide range covering most of the JOA. The introduction of rover units allowed SOF teams in the field to receive the UAV feed and transmit valuable intelligence to their Philippine counterparts. Small UAVs, such as the Raven and Aqua Puma, also supported fielded units.

These ISR assets remained under the control of U.S. forces, but the intelligence gained from them was processed and then shared with the appropriate echelon of the Philippine forces carrying out the operations. Figure 5.3 depicts the agreed-upon process for collecting, fusing, and sharing intelligence with the PSF. Over the course of OEF-P, the type, number, and capability of the ISR platforms varied, and some were supplied through contract while others were assigned or organic assets, but the basic system for information-sharing remained the same.

### Improving Air Support to Ground Operations

Among JSOTF-P's various elements, none played a more varied and consequential role than the PAF LCE. Its mission was to "advise and assist the Philippine Air Force (PAF) to build a combat effective counterinsurgency capability" aimed at defeating terrorist organizations in the JOA (PAF LCE, 2012, slide 3). The PAF LCE was not always fully manned, but its organizational structure included an AFSOC team lead, a fixed-wing close air support officer, two rotary-wing experts, a combat controller, and two intelligence experts. The team lead was a pilot from AFSOC's 6th Special Operations Squadron, which specializes in training foreign air forces. Over time, the PAF LCE developed deep ties with not only the 3rd Air Division elements based at Zamboanga (Edwin Andrews Air Base) but with the 15th Strike Wing at U.S. Naval Station Sangley Point, the 710 Special Operations Wing at Crow

**Figure 5.2**
**U.S. Government and Contract Resources Provided to Joint Special Operations Task Force—Philippines**

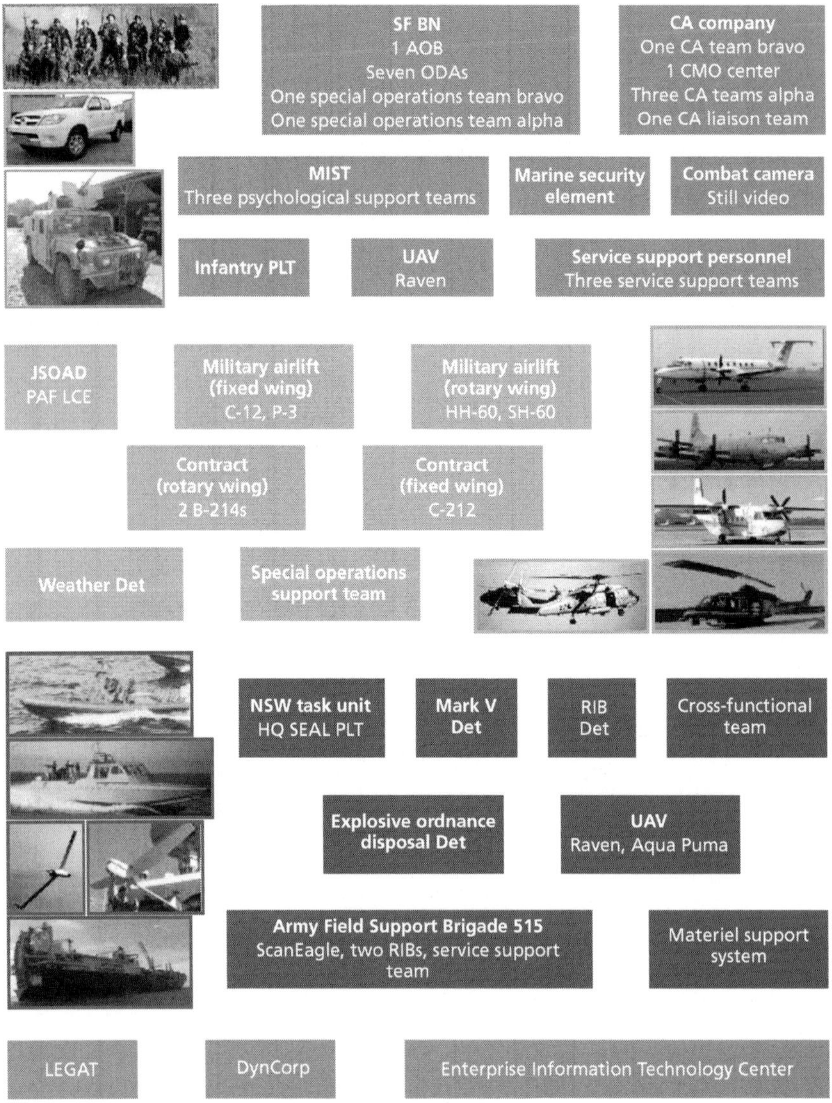


SOURCE: JSOTF-P, 2008b, slide 6.
NOTE: JSOAD = Joint Special Operations Air Detachment.
RAND *RR1236-5.2*

**Figure 5.3**
**Information-Gathering and Sharing**

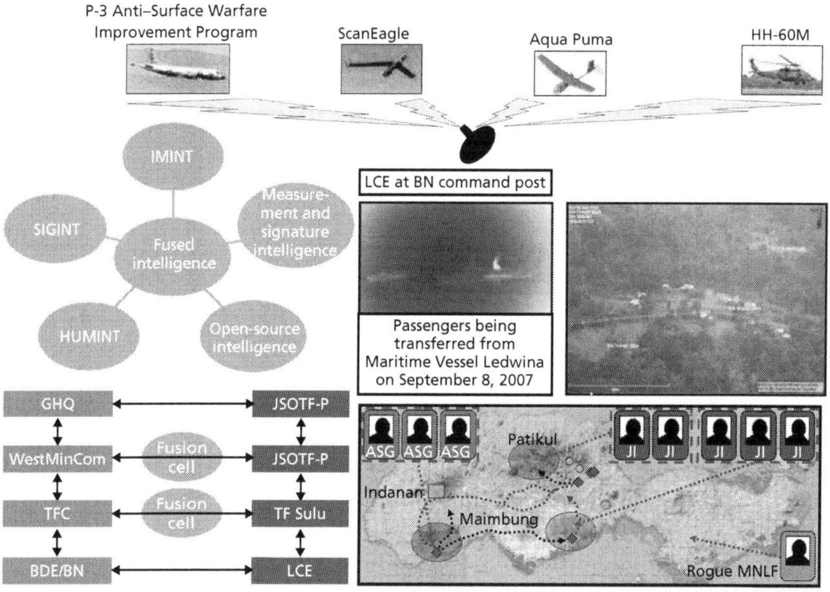


SOURCE: JSOTF-P, 2008b, slide 18.
RAND *RR1236-5.3*

Valley Range, and tactical operations groups throughout the JOA and Cebu (interview 31, October 9, 2014).

The PAF's once-substantial capability had degraded significantly because of declining defense spending. Only one of three C-130s in its fleet was operable, and its strike platforms were old and limited in number. The PAF LCE found that there was no written doctrine to support many functions, including CASEVAC and MEDEVAC, so it provided doctrine and taught classes. Since 2006, the PAF LCE taught an air–ground coordination course to Philippine airmen, and, in 2007, the PAF graduated and deployed its first forward air controllers to operations in Jolo and Basilan. The PAF LCE also trained SOF teams in battle-damage assessment and sensitive-site exploitation. It also trained Philippine helicopter pilots in night-vision flying, as well as CASEVAC. The PAF LCE was the lead element in training OV-10 crews in both phases of the upgraded strike capability, the transition from dumb to fuzed bombs, and then on the tactics and equipment for the Section 1206 program to provide the PAF with a precision-strike capability. The U.S. team assisted the PAF in developing the capability for two different platforms, the OV-10 and the S-211. The S-211 strike wing commander sought out the PAF LCE for various other types of advice.

The experience and the expertise of the PAF LCE members earned the team significant credibility with the PAF units and commanders. The team included F-16 and Apache pilots with multiple combat tours in Afghanistan and Iraq. Their advice was sought on a range of matters, including use of lasers and forward-looking infrared and the types of platforms and simulators that should be purchased. Unfortunately, some of this advice did not result in foreign military sales cases, and new planes were purchased without the requisite training and spare parts, as was a helicopter with features not suitable for combat.

## Summary

JSOTF-P adapted its efforts in 2008–2010 to respond to a shifting and increased threat in some locations, as well as deficits in AFP capabilities. The new commander also adopted a more decentralized approach by delegating authority to plan operations and allocate resources to subordinate TFs, TF Sulu, TF Archipelago, and TF Mindanao. He also increased IO.

Attacks across the provinces where the ASG was most active dropped during this period, as Figure 5.4 shows. They decreased from 29 in Basilan in 2008 to 19 there in 2009 and 25 in 2010. In Sulu, there were 23 enemy-initiated attacks in 2008, 41 in 2009, and a decline to 15 in 2010. The number of enemy-initiated attacks occurring on Tawi-Tawi remained relatively low and constant, with a slight drop in 2009. Although the ASG and JI were present in central Mindanao, the MILF conducted the majority of armed attacks there.

The increased violence and threat activities in Mindanao led JSOTF-P to expand its efforts in that area in support of the AFP. Increased mapping of the central Mindanao environment, including

**Figure 5.4**
**Enemy-Initiated Incidents in Basilan, Sulu, and Tawi-Tawi, 2008–2010**

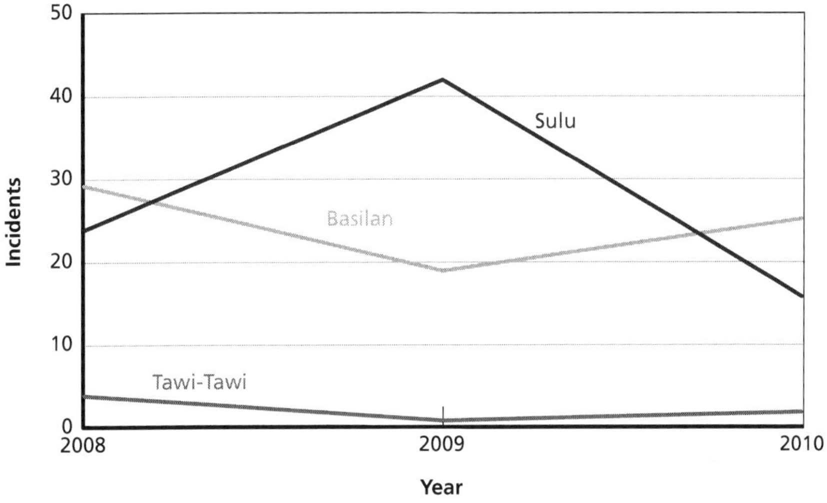


SOURCE: ESOC data.
NOTE: Incidents are counts of enemy-initiated incidents per year by province.
RAND *RR1236-5.4*

emergent threat groups, led to a greater understanding of the interactions among all threat groups. Training, advice, intelligence support, CMO, and MEDEVAC aided AFP operations that targeted permitted threat groups and increased the capabilities of the AFP units. On Basilan, AFP units achieved a new maturity in operations to deal with violence there, and, in the Sulu archipelago, JSOTF-P exercised leverage to address the political–military aspects of the threat. The violence in Sulu declined to the lowest levels since 2002 (ESOC, undated).[3]

As the formal assessment conducted by USPACOM in 2008 indicated, the JSOTF-P activities might have begun to reach the point of culmination on Basilan and Jolo. The Mindanao environment continued to be a safe haven for transnational threat groups, but the upsurge in fighting with MILF factions created some limitations on the type of support the JSOTF-P could provide because its mission was limited

[3] See Figure 8.1 in Chapter Eight of the present report.

to groups with transnational linkages. The continuing U.S. support to the AFP enabled ongoing improvements in its capabilities, however, and CMO and IO produced beneficial effects in terms of population support and threat conditions.

Some of the JSOTF-P initiatives to provide the AFP with a precision-targeting capability to fix and finish high-value targets of the targeted armed groups bore fruit during this time frame, including the transition to fuzed bombs, with a resulting increase in effectiveness. Enhanced intelligence support to operations and broadened support to PAF elements resulted in increased effectiveness and new capabilities, including CASEVAC and forward air control. The AFP also expanded its CMO and increased its capability thanks to more-comprehensive and decentralized JSOTF-P methods, with a resulting increase in population support for the AFP and GRP. Several of the initiatives begun in this period did not bear fruit until subsequent years.

CHAPTER SIX

# 2010–2012: Transitioning Up

The period of 2010 to 2012 was marked by major national planning initiatives by the Philippine government that provided new guidance for Philippine national security strategy and AFP institutional development.

The Internal Peace and Security Plan (IPSP) Bayanihan, released in early 2010, adopted a "multi-stakeholder approach" to peace and security in the Philippines. The IPSP mandated that, by 2016, responsibility for internal security would transition from the AFP to the PNP. The IPSP also identified the Filipino people as the most-important stakeholders in ensuring peace and security, which created an imperative to form a shared concept of security with the Filipino population. The IPSP stated that winning the peace is not purely a military solution but rather requires a whole-of-nation approach, with the security forces and government institutions working together with civil societies and communities to share responsibility in developing a lasting security and peace (AFP, 2010). Plan Samahan, published on July 11, 2011, was the sister plan for the PNP, outlining a phased approach to assuming the lead for internal security by 2016 (interview 20, October 6, 2014). The Philippine Army (PA) released *Army Transformation Roadmap 2028*, which is the PA's 18-year strategic vision to modernize and upgrade its capabilities (HQ, PA, undated).

In response to these new directives, JSOTF-P took steps to integrate its plans with GRP national-level plans and to shift the weight of its advisory effort from tactical level to higher HQ and institutional development. Specifically, JSOTF-P adapted its effort to include an intensive effort to train special police forces, to integrate them with the military's current operations per the IPSP, and to refocus its various AFP capability-building efforts to ensure that they would be sustainable after OEF-P ended. Three successive JSOTF-P commanders continued this focus on higher-level operational and institutional development.

In 2010, a USPACOM assessment concluded that it was time for the U.S. military to begin planning to bring OEF-P to a close. DoD concurred with the recommendation. In response, JSOTF-P began a combined planning effort with the U.S. country team, which would inherit the lead role for post–OEF-P U.S. assistance, to ensure that its current activities and plans were consistent with U.S. mission plans.

## Assessment and Adaptation

In 2010, USPACOM conducted a comprehensive assessment of the OEF-P campaign at the request of the USPACOM commander. This assessment followed the approach of the 2008 USPACOM assessment, which evaluated progress according to OEF-P mission orders, which had been updated in 2005. The assessment found that OEF-P had achieved sufficient results; it was submitted to the Joint Chiefs of Staff, who then shared it with the Office of the Secretary of Defense. In response, DoD issued a memorandum mandating that planning to end the mission in incremental fashion commence, with a projected end to OEF-P as a named operation by the end of FY 2015 (interview 16, October 3, 2014).

CAPT Robert V. Gusentine succeeded Coultrup as JSOTF-P commander on July 2, 2010. Gusentine, a U.S. Navy SEAL, arrived in the Philippines from SOCPAC, where he had served as the J-3, so he was already familiar with the OEF-P mission. After undertaking an initial 60-day assessment of the mission, he developed a plan to bring the JSOTF-P mission and activities into closer alignment with the country team and the AFP. Early in his tour, all of the JSOTF-P principal national-level interlocutors changed: Harry K. Thomas succeeded Kenney as ambassador, a new USAID director arrived, and a new AFP chief of staff was named. Gusentine and his deputy commander worked to develop positive relationships with all of them. In addition to ensuring that all JSOTF-P efforts linked to the national-level plans, Gusentine devoted particular effort to linking CA activities to USAID's programs and to developing AFP CA capability (interview 51, October 24, 2014).

COL Francis M. Beaudette assumed command of JSOTF-P on June 24, 2011, shortly after the DoD guidance had been released. He focused heavily on initiating the transition. In his first 60 days of command, Colonel Beaudette conducted a troop-to-task analysis to "right-size" the force and conducted an assessment. Over the course of his tour, he reduced JSOTF-P manning by 200 troops, and he revised his lines of effort to include the need to integrate and support "friendly networks," including the U.S. country team and relevant Philippine entities. He also refocused JSOTF-P's AFP capacity-building line of effort on supporting joint and interagency integration at higher-level HQ, including military–police coordination (interview 72, August 14, 2013).

In 2011, JSOTF-P offered personnel to support the State Department's analysis using the Interagency Conflict Assessment Framework, which provided the embassy with a current understanding of the situation in Mindanao to inform its planning process. JSOTF-P incorporated the Interagency Conflict Assessment Framework findings into its own plan. To coordinate implementation of these plans, the embassy created its key integrating mechanism, the Mindanao Working Group, which brought together all entities on the country team involved in Mindanao and JSOTF-P. Led by the deputy chief of mission Leslie A. Bassett, the working group developed the Mindanao Engagement Strategy, which outlined JSOTF-P's supporting role for State Department efforts in Mindanao (interview 62, October 31, 2014). The working group provided a more formal integrating mechanism than had existed previously, raising interagency synergy to a new level. JSOTF-P provided support and force protection for working-group visits to the south.

COL Mark A. Miller took command of JSOTF-P on June 28, 2012, and conducted a 30-day assessment on behalf of SOCPAC. His primary conclusion was that stability and security in the southern Philippines would be achieved not by military means but through political measures. He therefore reinforced efforts to connect the U.S. military plans to those of the embassy and USAID because the transition plan envisioned that responsibility for security activities would migrate from JSOTF-P to the U.S. country team and the State Department's lead (interview 52, November 3, 2014).

Informed by the GRP plans, Colonel Miller worked with Philippine SOF leadership to emphasize their own institutional training capacity. His goal was to eliminate repetitive U.S. Subject Matter Expert Exchanges that taught the same skills over and over. The new approach aimed to create a permanent knowledge base within the AFP and a training capability that would allow for progressively less U.S. involvement (Oakley, 2014). Miller also focused efforts on developing the Philippine SOF capability and reduced operational support to field units while continuing the emphasis on IO and CMO, especially on central Mindanao, where the transnational terrorist threat had increased (interview 52, November 3, 2014).

## Plan Execution

### Synchronizing with Embassy and Government of the Republic of the Philippines Plans

Starting in 2010, the JSOTF-P deputy commanding officer devoted most of his time to synchronizing JSOTF-P efforts with the embassy and engaging with the Philippine military at GHQ. The deputy commanding officer served as the primary conduit for all JSOTF-P information flows to the country team. Throughout this period, the JSOTF-P commander and his key staff typically spent five days per week at Camp Navarro and two days in Manila for meetings at the embassy and with Philippine officials at the national level. This continued until 2013, when the ratio was reversed, and the commander began to spend five days in Manila and two days in Zamboanga.

JSOTF-P's relationship with the U.S. interagency community, particularly USAID, also deepened over time, although perspectives differed as to the extent. Some interviewees stressed the increasing coordination of JSOTF-P and USAID, while others criticized USAID's distance from the projects it was managing (interview 50, October 24, 2014; interview 70, December 3, 2014). Some at the U.S. embassy believed that JSOTF-P conducted redundant survey work and did not rely sufficiently on USAID and embassy expertise (interview 65, December 15, 2014). However, both civilian and military interviewees agreed that the relationship was strengthened after Gloria D. Steele arrived as USAID mission director in 2010. Her staff and JSOTF-P worked to coordinate USAID's strategy and mission plan with JSOTF-P's ability to support them. She realigned the geographic areas of focus with the six conflict-affected areas in which JSOTF-P was operating so that USAID and JSOTF-P's efforts would be integrated and mutually reinforcing (interview 23, October 7, 2014).

JSOTF-P placed a liaison officer (LNO) at USAID in Manila, and, beginning in fall 2013, a full-time USAID LNO was embedded with JSOTF-P in Zamboanga to help with coordination efforts. This full-time connectivity enabled constant coordination and communication. Generally, JSOTF-P focuses on small-scale projects with more-immediate impacts (such as MEDCAPs and veterinary civic action programs [VETCAPs]), whereas USAID projects tend to be longer term, such as the GEM project (interview 23, October 7, 2014). JSOTF-P's engineering assets allowed it to contribute to infrastructure projects. For example, at the area coordination center on Jolo, JSOTF-P funded the building, and USAID provided the teachers and supplies. Finally, both civilian and military U.S. officials said that JSOTF-P personnel provided crucial support in monitoring USAID projects because of their constant travels around the JOA (interview 24, October 7, 2014; interview 32, October 10, 2014).

### Focusing on the Operational Level and Institution-Building

JSOTF-P focused in this period on developing capability at higher HQ of both the Philippine SOF and AFP joint commands, as well as supporting institutional development. The JSOTF-P advisory teams, known as LCEs and functional coordination elements, for institutional development were redistributed to higher-level HQ to perform these roles. A team placed at AFP HQ provided information to the distributed SOF network, as well as AFP leadership in the field, remedying a longstanding dearth of information flowing to and from the senior leaders in Manila to the remote southern Philippines (interview 72, August 14, 2013; interview 42, October 3, 2014).[1] This information flow enabled the leaders to connect the strategic, operational, and tactical levels of effort.

To improve C2 of operations in the southern Philippines, JSOTF-P took several steps to develop higher-level operational coordination among all PSF entities. Interviewees noted that commanders of conventional forces, SOF, PNP SAF, and other units, such as the Presidential Security Group did not routinely coordinate planning and operations (interview 17, October 6, 2014; interview 30, October 9, 2014). JSOTF-P built and advised nine fusion cells in Mindanao, Basilan, and Jolo to enable police–military coordination and intelligence fusion (interview 73, August 14, 2013).

JSOTF-P also assisted Philippine SOF to improve their operational and institutional HQ structures.

The Joint SOG (JSOG) was created as an operational command for joint operations by the light reaction units and naval special operations units. The JSOG is a national mission force and falls under the command of the AFP chief of staff. Unified commands, such as WestMinCom, request JSOG forces from AFP GHQ and then place them under the command of the conventional JTF commander (interview 43, October 9, 2014). The Philippine SOF leader, when he deployed to the field, would act as an adviser to the joint commander rather than command his own forces (interview 33, October 10, 2014). Although AFP employment of SOF had improved over the years, the development of deployable SOF command HQ was deemed desirable to improve planning and execution of operations.

[1] See also "Partnered Counterterrorism Operations in the Philippines," 2011, pp. 9–10, which found that, during the period of research, neither JSOTF-P nor the U.S. country-team programs placed sufficient emphasis on institutional development to create a sustainable capability. The report specifically mentions the U.S. Department of Justice's International Criminal Investigative Training Assistance Program as lacking an institutional focus.

To build these command and control and other capabilities, U.S. SOF established advisory cells at every Philippine SOF command headquarters. For years, JSOTF-P had trained and advised Philippine SOF at its bases in Luzon. In this period, TF North, the U.S. SF company at the SOCOM PA and Light Reaction Regiment (LRR) HQ in Fort Magsaysay, elevated its focus to institutional development, including C2 structures; functions, including equipping and resource management; and force generation. In 2013, the LRR was ordered to double in size, from three to six companies, in a year's time, so assisting the LRR's expansion and related HQ needs became the TF North's top priority (interviews 28 and 29, October 8, 2014). Philippine SOF officers described the numerous HQ staffing, resource, and training needs (interview 29, October 8, 2014). In the spring of 2013, JSOTF-P helped create a SOF Center of Excellence at SOCOM PA, which coordinated the U.S. SOF enduring and episodic training efforts; refined Philippine SOF unit requirements, standards, and curricula; and eliminated redundancies in training capacity (Oakley, 2014).

#### *Philippine National Police Special Action Force*

As noted above, one of the central tenets of the IPSP was the main focus of the Filipino people on the peace and security effort. In doing so, it recognized the importance of transitioning to a police-led internal security focus, as well as the legitimacy of such an internal security force. This new directive led JSOTF-P to prioritize military–police coordination and advisory assistance to the PNP SAF.

JSOTF-P began working with the newly formed PNP SAF in 2008, but an enduring advise-and-assist relationship was not developed until 2011 (interview 20, October 6, 2014), when Colonel Beaudette sent an ODA to advise the PNP HQ at Camp Aguinaldo. To galvanize information-sharing and military–police coordination, Beaudette set up eight fusion centers in various Mindanao subregions. At these centers, U.S. SOF shared U.S. intelligence and encouraged military and police intelligence elements to share as well. Although the AFP and PNP balked at first, over time, the coordination increased. The PNP SAF and AFP Marine Corps began cross-training each other in skills they did not have. Beaudette also opened up the JSOTF-P

Joint Operations Center to Filipino police and military representatives, and they would come in to help plan and review operations, which greatly strengthened the relationship between all entities (interview 72, August 14, 2013).

A common sentiment was that the police would not be ready to take over internal security by 2016 as outlined in the IPSP (interview 19, October 6, 2014; interview 43, October 9, 2014; interview 30, October 9, 2014). This transition is recognized as requiring a great deal more time and resources invested in the PNP and PNP SAF to develop sufficient capabilities to allow them to take over internal security—some estimated another ten years (interview 19, October 6, 2014). Although considered a very competent urban force, PNP SAF do not get the resource support that the AFP receives. In addition, the PNP recruits locally, has very few good leaders, and no good middle management or leadership to grow in the ranks. Finally, when compared with the AFP, JSOG members are trained experts in urban operations, and SOCOM PA has the depth of leadership and expertise that PNP SAF just does not have (interview 19, October 6, 2014).

The PNP SAF grew to six battalions, with three battalions based in Mindanao (interview 21, October 6, 2014). There is a six-month required foundational course for all PNP SAF, and then they are assigned to units for another six months of on-the-job field training. After a subsequent five-month commando training course, they are assigned to PNP SAF companies. Friction and rivalry between the police and military have been cited as common. Much of this has to do with the overlap in mission sets, resourcing problems, and lack of strategic direction to delineate responsibilities between services. The JSOG has an urban mission set and is better resourced and equipped than the PNP SAF. However, the PNP SAF are supposed to have primacy in urban environments. This leads to coordination issues, but, ultimately, PNP SAF units deploy in support of AFP-planned and -run operations, so they ultimately fall under the AFP commander (interview 20, October 6, 2014).

PNP SAF are generally seen as a capable force, but they are trained to operate only in urban environments, which limits their reach and effectiveness in certain operations. They were not trained to operate in the jungle environments of Basilan and Jolo, for example. PNP SAF capability improved over time, however, and, beginning in early 2009, units were deployed to Jolo, Basilan, and northeast Mindanao.

### *Precision-Strike Capability*

The program to give the Philippine air force a precision-strike capability reached a milestone in 2012 (interview 36; October 10, 2014). The assistance, authorized under the FY 2010 NDAA Section 1206, provided $18.4 million of equipment and training to give the PAF OV-10s a precision-strike capability; the letter of acceptance of the precision-guided munition program was received in July 2010, and the next year and a half consisted of equipment installation, munition training, initial test drops, and validation of software (DoD, 2012a).[2] The first use of the capability occurred on February 2, 2012, according to Philippine officials, who said that the program was the fruit of extended efforts by the AFP, JSOTF-P, and other U.S. agencies.[3]

---

[2] The "USPACOM Data Roll-up" section on p. 118 shows $18.4 million for the Philippines for FY 2010 under Section 1206 authority:

> Close Air Support/Precision Guided Munitions Capability. This program gave the Philippines Armed Forces (AFP) the capability to deliver swift precision strikes against identified terrorist leadership. Moreover, it significantly reduces the chance of collateral damage and civilian casualties. Designed to train the AFP to provide a means to target terrorists hiding in remote areas and operating from sanctuaries presently unreachable due to early warning networks. This program included the Enhanced Paveway program, upgrades for 5 OV-10 Bronco ACs, Radios, TALON ground radios, Night Vision Devices, M4 Carbine, AN/PEQ-2A Infrared Aiming Lasers.

[3] DoD, 2012b, p. 28 states,

> D. USPACOM—Summary of successful projects.
>
> 1. Section 1206, Philippines: In FY10, the U.S. Air Force and its Office of International Affairs (SAF/IA) undertook an aggressive Section 1206 effort to equip existing Philippines Air Force OV-10 aircraft with Enhanced Paveway II precision guided munitions kits. Receiving funding in January 2010, this complex capability completed significant testing in August 2011, which demonstrated its initial capability. Completing final testing in January 2011, the Armed Forces of the Philippines (AFP) employed this new capability immediately—with significant results. On 2 February 2012, the Philippines pilots engaged and destroyed an encampment containing multiple high value targets in the troubled Sulu Archipelago. This engagement was a major turning point in the decade long struggle against the Abu Sayaf Group and Jemaah Islamiya. Additionally, this engagement represented a significant leap in the AFP capability. Moreover, this

According to a Philippine general who was closely involved in the program, the AFP considered it a success because forces successfully coordinated and dropped the bombs on the designated site within the prescribed range, although the primary target did escape (interview 36; October 10, 2014). The AFP made statements to the media about the success of that operation, using it as an IO campaign to exploit the good news (see, for example, "Philippines Using US Smart Bombs," 2012).[4] In addition, AFP CMO efforts commenced shortly thereafter in that geographic area, to mitigate the impact and reinforce relations with the local population (interview 8, October 2, 2014).

Despite numerous bureaucratic delays, the operation was deemed a successful culmination of two years' work; after the strike, the ASG told the JI to leave Jolo and distanced itself from the group (interview 37, October 10, 2014; interview 63, December 6, 2014).

### Institutionalizing an Armed Forces of the Philippines Civil Affairs Capability

CMO matured over the course of OEF-P for several reasons. In the earlier years, the AFP did not value or emphasize CMO, and some of JSOTF-P's CA efforts in the southern Philippines were wrongheaded or redundant. For example, humanitarian projects in Jolo in 2005–2006 were focused primarily on building schools, without understanding that schools already existed in abundance on Jolo and that nearly every village on the island had a school (Daniels, 2009). Senior U.S. civilians observed that USAID and the embassy's political and economic sections had deep subject-matter expertise that JSOTF-P did not tap in the early years. Nonetheless, CA activities did secure tactical access and population sentiment in both Basilan and Jolo, which can contribute to strategic objectives. For example, during Operation Ultimatum in 2006, despite AFP reluctance to enter the area between

---

engagement went a long way toward validating the 1206 model of combining accelerated funding, rapidly adaptable technology, close partnership, and focused training, all for maximum effects.

[4] The Philippine press reported extensively on the airstrike based on Philippine military officials' statements, including the initial claim that "Marwan," a JI leader, had been killed in the attack along with two other senior ASG figures.

Jolo City and the MNLF camp, JSOTF-P CA enlisted the support of the mayor to conduct MEDCAPs, VETCAPs, and dental civic action programs.

The AFP observed CMO's positive effects on gaining the support of the population and began emulating the model, according to both U.S. and Philippine interviewees (interview 41, October 11, 2014; interview 58, November 14, 2014; interview 22, October 7, 2014). AFP CMO began in earnest under General Juancho Sabban, when he was TF Comet commander from 2007 to 2009. He modeled AFP CMO efforts after those of JSOTF-P CA teams (interview 25, October 7, 2014). General Sabban emphasized the focus of CMO on gaining the support of the population, with the central concept of winning the peace. He hand-selected commanders who understood the importance of CMO; Sabban's successor as TF Comet commander continued his heavy emphasis on CMO in Jolo; indeed, he continued to support civil society leaders and development in Jolo after his retirement and in continuing service as a senior civilian official (interview 22, October 7, 2014).

Sabban also worked with the United States to set up the AFP CMO school (interview 47, November 10, 2014). The AFP Civil Relations Service consists of small elements that are attached to conventional army units. The AFP's "triad" of Civil Relations Service specialization consists of CMO, public affairs operations, and Information Support Affairs (equivalent to U.S. MISO). This often means that a single person would combine duties and be dual- or triple-hatted in positions in the unit (interview 32, October 9, 2014). The Philippine Army has a CMO group, and there is one CMO company per battalion. The Philippine Navy and Marine Corps have CMO groups as well, and every brigade has a CA team of about 15 to 20 people (interview 35, October 10, 2014).

Two AFP CMO schools exist—a joint school at Camp Aguinaldo, which supports unified commands, and a Philippine Army school in Bonifacio that trains forces for CMO units. The attendees do not become CA specialists as in the United States because the AFP does not have a CA military occupational specialty. Rather, soldiers go through the school and receive the specialization before being deployed to certain areas. This means that an AFP soldier could go through the CMO school but go back to another unit and do something entirely different (interview 69, November 12, 2014). Although the CMO school was created in early 2008, it took some time and experience of the soldiers coming out of the school to develop a fluency and capacity at conducting effective CMO. JSOTF-P CA teams helped develop courses and doctrine for the CMO school (interview 57, November 13, 2014).

The U.S. CA footprint and disposition fluctuated over time. CA was the only activity that JSOTF-P could conduct unilaterally and in combination with the AFP. As a result, four-person CA teams had more freedom of movement and activity (interview 69, November 12, 2014). In 2006, there were three JSOTF-P CA teams: two on Jolo and one in Mindanao. The CA teams lived and worked daily with their AFP counterparts and conducted joint key-leader engagements with Philippine officials and local influencers. The synergy benefited from the AFP's knowledge of the area and nature of the threat, which, in turn, made U.S. CA activities more effective (interview 58, November 14, 2014). In 2008, JSOTF-P CA presence increased to five CA teams and expanded its presence to Tawi-Tawi, Jolo, Basilan, Cotabato, Davao, and Zamboanga.

The CA effort evolved from a focus on tactical activities, such as MEDCAPs and VETCAPs, and, from 2008 onward, U.S. CA began to conduct Subject Matter Expert Exchanges aimed at the operational level as AFP CMO units became more capable at the tactical level (interview 57, November 13, 2014). The CA teams not only worked with the AFP CMO teams on the ground but also assisted with developing capacity at the CMO school in Manila. They provided instructors and helped develop the curriculum to educate junior AFP officers on the value and importance of CMO in gaining the support of the population.

During Gusentine's tour as JSOTF-P commander, he emphasized AFP CMO capabilities and work, which increased the trust and confidence of the population (interview 36, October 11, 2014). He worked closely with Brig. Gen. Carlito Galvez to complete the ring road around Basilan using JSOTF-P, USAID, and AFP CMO assets.

Completing this project would extend access and security to its remotest areas (interview 50, October 24, 2014; interview 70, December 3, 2014).

In sum, U.S. SOF prioritized CMO activities and, over the course of OEF-P, conducted many thousands of activities. By their accounts, these reaped a great deal of tactical access and information from the population; in addition, independent polls show a decrease in the population's support for the ASG, which suggests that U.S. SOF achieved some measure of strategic success in denying the ASG access to population support, resources, and safe haven (Teutsch and Thambidurai, 2014). But, with limited U.S. CA assets (three to five four-person CA teams), the longest-lasting impact of CMO was the AFP's enthusiastic adoption of CMO and its creation of a sustainable capability to produce troops trained in CMO. In later years, U.S. SOF and USAID made efforts to ensure that projects were not redundant and were serving legitimate economic development needs. This study did not evaluate project-level results or the overall impact on economic development, but undoubtedly some number of roads, schools, wells, and other structures were built that were not needed, finished, or maintained. Special inspectors general in both Iraq and Afghanistan amply documented such problems, although the levels of U.S. expenditure in the Philippines were far lower (see, for example, the quarterly reports of the Special Inspector General for Afghanistan Reconstruction, undated).

### Measuring Progress

During this period, JSOTF-P sought additional means to evaluate and verify the effects that it was achieving or not achieving. Two new methods were introduced to provide further evidence to support such evaluations. First, to gauge the threat, and informed by guidance from the SOCPAC commander, JSOTF-P developed a tool to measure progress based on concrete measures that showed reduced space for ASG operations and recruitment activity. "Heat charts" depicted the threat evolution through measures, such as roads that could be traversed by different groups, and provided a simple and transparent method to evaluate the level of security in different areas (interview 52, November 3, 2014; interview 53, November 6, 2014).

Second, to gauge the population sentiment with regard to both the armed groups and the government, another important assessment capability was introduced in 2012. A team of analysts began conducting a comprehensive quarterly survey called the Southern Philippines Public Perception Survey. These polls registered the population's perceptions in six conflict zones—Zamboanga, Basilan, Isabela City, Cotabato, Jolo, and Marawi City (interview 72, August 14, 2013). Survey results were shared with WestMinCom, senior AFP officials, the mayor of Zamboanga City, and the U.S. country team. The survey provided a new way to evaluate progress, identify issues important to the population of the southern Philippines, and adjust plans and programs (interview 5, October 2, 2014).

Anecdotal evidence also mounted that AFP CMO were contributing to the reduction in the threat level and the increase in population support for the government. Because of the AFP role in providing health, education, and other services in remote areas and protecting villages from attack, the AFP was increasingly viewed as the defender of previously neglected populations (interview 58, November 14, 2014).

JSOTF-P assessed that the JI threat had been degraded and the ASG had been reduced to a low-grade criminal threat focused primarily on kidnap for ransom (interview 51, October 24, 2014). A generally sustained downward trend in enemy-initiated attacks (see Figure 6.1) and the continued reduction of operational space and support for armed groups supported the thesis that the combination of combat operations, CMO, and civilian programs to address basic needs was succeeding.

## Summary

During 2010–2012, JSOTF-P undertook numerous efforts to enable the Philippine government to sustain progress and institutionalize the security force capabilities in advance of the expected U.S. transition and end to the mission. The command also brought earlier efforts to fruition as it began the initial transition planning and activities. These activities and their corresponding outcomes are enumerated below.

JSOTF-P integrated its plans with those of the U.S. embassy country team and the Philippine government to achieve greater synergy and plan for the hand-off of efforts to those two entities. JSOTF-P devoted particular effort to achieving closer collaboration with USAID. It also began detailed planning and deliberate reductions of JSOTF-P staff. The integrating efforts gave both the U.S. embassy and senior Philippine officials and ministries greater visibility of the operations in the south and capability and resource requirements. The Manila government took steps to address those needs.

The bulk of JSOTF-P support to AFP capacity-building during this period shifted from the tactical level to operational HQ and institutional development. Higher-level planning and intelligence fusion and institutional development were seen as the keys to a sustainable AFP capability. Such capabilities were created, including an opera-

**Figure 6.1**
**Enemy-Initiated Incidents in Basilan, Sulu, and Tawi-Tawi, 2010–2012**

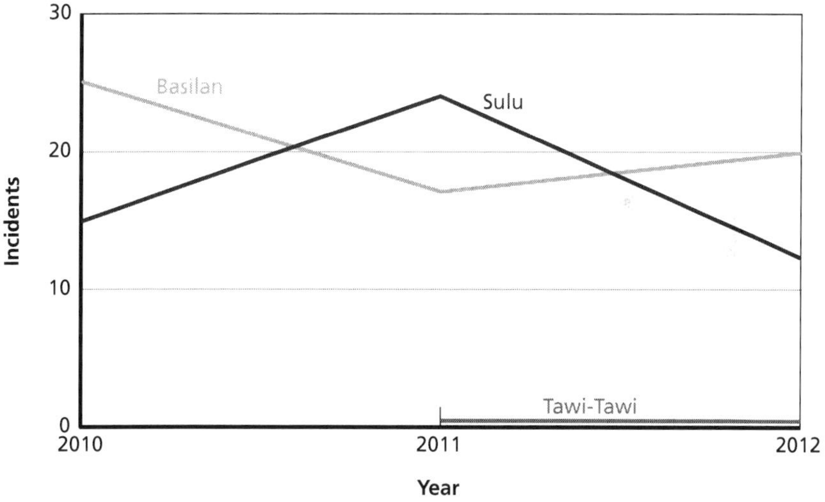


SOURCE: ESOC data.
NOTE: Incidents are counts of enemy-initiated incidents per year by province.
RAND *RR1236-6.1*

tions center at WestMinCom to enhance joint operations, and schools, courses, and doctrine for CMO. Philippine SOF institutional and C2 capabilities were also improved.

The Philippine government's release of a national plan, the IPSP, prompted JSOTF-P to take several actions in support of its implementation. It began training, advising, and equipping national police special units to prepare for the transfer of internal security responsibilities to the police. It built and supported fusion cells for military–police coordination. And it increased efforts in support of a whole-of-society approach to security.

Finally, the program to provide a precision-strike capability came to fruition in this period. The AFP's ability to sustain this capability remained uncertain following a crash in 2013 that cost the life of the most experienced PAF pilot. The OV-10 fleet was grounded, but the program later resumed with the S-211 platform (interview 54, October 27, 2014). In addition, the Philippine government made significant investments in weapons and new air platforms that would eventually increase capability. The overall development of AFP capability had reached a point, according to official assessments, at which it could successfully confront the threats in the southern Philippines. Ongoing corruption, collusion, and lack of investment in essential services were continuing factors limiting success.

In terms of kinetics, attacks generally dropped on Basilan and Sulu from 2010 to 2012. On Basilan, attacks dropped from 25 to 20 during this period. On Sulu, they dropped from 24 in 2011 to 12 in 2012.

CHAPTER SEVEN

# 2012–2014: Zamboanga Siege and Transitioning Out

In 2013, two major, unexpected events slowed progress toward the transition. The Zamboanga siege in September involved an insurgent assault and a prolonged hostage crisis in one of the Philippines' largest and densest urban littoral environments. Two months later, a devastating typhoon hit the southern Philippines and pressed the small JSOTF-P into emergency relief assistance activities as the only nearby U.S. force with desperately needed knowledge, medical and CA expertise, equipment, and transport.

The final two JSOTF-P commanders oversaw the final phases of OEF-P, the drawdown and closure of JSOTF-P and the transfer of all follow-on missions to the PAT, a SOF element housed in the U.S. embassy. To this end, JSOTF-P prioritized institutional development, as well as interagency coordination, so that both the PSF and the U.S. interagency community would be able to sustain and continue the gains.

Two agreements promised to affect the final transition of OEF-P. In 2014, the GRP concluded a major agreement with the United States, the Enhanced Defense Cooperation Agreement (GRP and United States, 2014), which envisioned ongoing and expanded U.S. security cooperation as the OEF-P mission ended. In addition, the government reached a peace accord with the MILF, the Comprehensive Agreement on the Bangsamoro (CAB) (Government of the Philippines and MILF, 2014). If implemented successfully, the CAB offered the prospect of reducing or ending the long-running armed separatist movement in the south. The JSOTF-P planners sought to prepare for transition amid the possible implementation of the CAB—as well as the possibility that splinter factions might reject the accord and continue fighting.

## Assessment and Adaptation

JSOTF-P sought to ensure that the stage was set for a successful transition. The first step was to transition to civilian authorities (Phase V, in U.S. joint doctrinal terms) and then to steady-state operations (Phase 0) after the projected conclusion of OEF-P on September 31, 2015. In July 2013, USPACOM ordered that the transition to Phase V be complete by May 2014. COL Robert C. McDowell took command of JSOTF-P on August 16, 2013. He believed that the JSOTF-P commander succeeding him should be an O-5 rank officer because of the declining size of the command, but it was eventually agreed that an O-6 officer was needed to interface effectively at the embassy and AFP GHQ level (interview 16, October 3, 2014). Colonel McDowell conducted an assessment to evaluate the AFP's institutional development and its ability to sustain the gains achieved over the previous 12 years. Using this information, he and his staff developed a transition plan, building on the work done by preceding commands. The plan was developed and briefed to the U.S. ambassador and USAID mission director, as well as Philippine Defense Secretary Voltaire T. Gazmin and the AFP chief of staff, and was signed in March 2014 (interview 44, September 30, 2014).

COL Erik M. Brown assumed command of JSOTF-P in May 2014 and inherited the transition plan that Colonel McDowell had created. His team conducted a 90-day assessment and proposed several adjustments to the existing transition plan. The most-significant adjustments entailed expanding the PAT's role and its tenure. He concluded that mobility assets should be retained, that the PAT tour of duty needed to be one year instead of six months, and that the PAT efforts would rely heavily on AFP partners and the U.S. interagency community. In addition, his 90-day assessment concluded that the AFP and PNP were primarily reactive in their operations in the southern Philippines and that PSF policies would need to take account of existing deficits in operational capabilities (interview 19, October 6, 2014; interview 33, October 10, 2014).

The Enhanced Defense Cooperation Agreement signed by the GRP and United States on April 28, 2014, envisioned an expanded bilateral partnership by increasing training and access of U.S. military forces to PSF military bases in order to assist with continued PSF development. It established the framework for enduring U.S. SOF training and assistance.[1]

Second, on March 27, 2014, the GRP and MILF leadership signed the CAB, which provided for enhanced autonomy in the Bangsamoro region. The Bangsamoro Basic Law was submitted to the Philippine Congress to be ratified, after which a plebiscite was to be held (Marcelo, 2014). The implementation of the accord would have a profound effect on the security situation in Mindanao, including the prospect that some splinter groups might continue to fight. The prospects for the accord were further clouded after 44 PNP SAF troops died in a clash with MILF rebels and the splinter Bangsamoro Islamic Freedom Fighters (BIFF) on January 25, 2015.[2] Officials later confirmed that the operation resulted in the death of Marwan, the top JI target in the country.[3] The MILF actions, the high death toll, and questions about the execution of the operation shelved consideration of the Bangsamoro Basic Law and led to the resignation of the PNP SAF commander. President Aquino's priority of advancing conflict resolution in the south appeared to be in jeopardy.

---

[1] The Philippines posted the agreement online (GRP and United States, 2014).

[2] "Policy Paralysis and Delays to Bangsamoro Basic Law Likely After Fighting Between Police and Militants in Philippines," 2015, reported that

> the 55th SAF Company blocking force and the 84th SAF Company seaborne unit were sent in to arrest Zulkifli bin Hir ("Marwan") and Basit Usman on suspicion of links to terrorist groups and making bombs, when they encountered the 105th Base Command of the MILF, which claims it was not notified of the operation, as required by existing cease-fire terms.

[3] *Marwan* is an alias; his real name was Zulkifli bin Hir.

## Plan Execution

### Zamboanga Siege

The Zamboanga siege occurred from September 9 to October 3, 2013. On September 9, about 400 armed elements of an MNLF faction dubbed "Rogue MNLF" converged on Zamboanga. Their declared intent was to reinforce an earlier declaration of independence from the GRP, ostensibly prompted by news of an impending peace agreement with the MILF, which would replace the ARMM with a new autonomous Bangsamoro entity in Mindanao.[4] As the rebels converged on the city, they took about 200 civilian hostages and began advancing toward a hospital and a school.

The AFP called for reinforcements to address the mushrooming crisis, and Philippine SOF, including JSOG and PNP SAF, were deployed to Zamboanga. The national security cabinet flew in to oversee the operation, and President Aquino spent nine days in Zamboanga personally supervising operations. The dense urban environment created an extremely complex battlefield; the PSF tried to avoid civilian casualties, clear segments of the city, and eventually capture or kill the MNLF members involved in the siege (interview 16, October 3, 2014; also Medina, 2013). A Philippine commander noted that the operational environment was extremely challenging because of the density of population and dwellings with no paths or streets between them, spreading fires, and displaced civilians (interview 35, October 10, 2014). As of the ninth day, most of the hostages had been rescued, had escaped, or had been released, but six were not rescued until September 27.

A total of 167 MNLF rebels, 23 government forces, and a dozen civilians were killed during the fighting; in addition, almost 120,000 residents were displaced by the conflict as large numbers of homes and other structures covering 344,000 square kilometers burned

---

[4] The basic facts are drawn from Philippine and U.S. SOF interviews 16, 20, and 36 and Medina, 2013.

down.[5] Human Rights Watch reported alleged abuses of detained rebel suspects, including children, and criticized the rebels for using civilians as human shields (Human Rights Watch, 2013). The watchdog group's annual report also criticized the government for its slow progress in moving tens of thousands of displaced and homeless people into housing more than a year after the crisis (Human Rights Watch, 2014). A subsequent government inquiry affirmed some of the allegations and ordered that charges be dropped against 60 of the 287 detainees for insufficient evidence (Alipala, 2014b).

Because the MNLF had carried out the attack rather than the ASG or JI, JSOTF-P was prevented from advising or assisting the AFP or PNP directly on the operation; the PSF conducted all operations unilaterally. However, JSOTF-P could undertake force-protection action measures because the fighting occurred a short distance from Camp Navarro. Thus, JSOTF-P was able to fly ISR, observe what was occurring on the ground, and advise WestMinCom on that basis (interview 16, October 3, 2014). During the siege, the PNP SAF LCE and JSOG LCE were also allowed to stay in touch with the units they had been advising (interview 37, October 10, 2014).

U.S. SOF observing the PSF response stated that the major roles were played by some 400 Philippine SOF, including the JSOG forces, which include LRR, the Scout Rangers, and the PNP SAF (interview 44, September 30, 2014; interview 41, October 11, 2014). They considered that the operation was the Philippine SOF's largest-scale and most effectively executed operation to date. President Aquino, who had monitored the operations from the JSOTF-P operations center, along with JSOG commander Dan Pamonag, PNP director Carmelo E. Valmoria, and LRR commander Ted Llamas, awarded medals to the Philippine SOF leadership. Conventional commanders overseeing the operation effectively employed Philippine SOF units, which had historically been a challenge within the AFP, and reportedly concluded from this experience that JSOG should henceforth be more

---

[5] The AFP totals differ slightly from those from the GMA News Online. According to Headquarters, WestMinCom, undated, 209 armed militants were killed, 294 captured, and 24 surrendered.

closely incorporated into AFP C2 structures (interview 37, October 10, 2014). The PNP and the PNP SAF were also employed as first responders because they possessed law enforcement powers to make arrests and collect evidence (interview 30, October 9, 2014).

An independent poll taken after the crisis ended showed that sentiment toward the MNLF had turned sharply negative; whereas previously only 5 percent of those surveyed said they felt threatened by the MNLF, as of November 2013, 33 percent of those in Mindanao and 60 percent of those in Zamboanga City said they felt threated by the MNLF.[6] Ninety-six percent of Zamboanga residents surveyed stated that they did not support the MNLF, and 74 percent of the Zamboanga residents agreed with the decision of the security forces to engage the MNLF, as did 51 percent of those in Mindanao. Sixty-one percent of Mindanao respondents said they were satisfied by the government response to the civilians affected by the crisis.

The U.S. SOF and Philippine officials interviewed considered that the PSF performance in the Zamboanga siege demonstrated the armed forces' ability to plan and execute joint operations in a complex environment at a sufficiently high level to validate the U.S. decision to end JSOTF-P. Nonetheless, it was not an unalloyed success. First, the government had been surprised by the attack and subsequent hostage-taking; the PSF had no advance knowledge through their intelligence networks. Also, delays due to a lack of PSF coordination reportedly prolonged operations (interview 19, October 8, 2014). The AFP, forced to employ all available and capable forces, sent in the SRR, which was not designed or trained to operate in an urban environment. The SRR adapted successfully, adopting tactics it observed the JSOG forces employing. A final deficit noted was insufficient forces to provide relief for the tactical units in the fight; units remained engaged around the clock for much of the standoff, often with insufficient resupply, which forced them to depend on the population for food and water (interview 29, October 8, 2014).

---

[6] Independent polling firm TNS Philippines conducted the surveys; poll results cited in this paragraph were reported in Teutsch and Thambidurai, 2014, pp. 63–68.

### Typhoon Yolanda

Less than two months later, another event occurred that diverted attention and resources from planning and executing the JSOTF-P drawdown. On November 8, 2013, category 5 Typhoon Haiyan (Yolanda) hit the central Philippines and devastated the areas in its path, killing an estimated 6,300 people and displacing about 6 million others (National Disaster Risk Reduction and Management Council, 2014). JSOTF-P personnel were the first to respond, employing their mobility and communication assets to help stage relief efforts. They provided assessment teams, assisted in opening airfields in the region to allow humanitarian aid to be flown into affected areas, coordinated with local government units, and helped establish coordination centers for humanitarian aid and rescue operations. As the first responder, JSOTF-P was able to assess the situation and report on areas most severely affected by the storm and supported the efforts of III Marine Expeditionary Force in conducting humanitarian assistance and disaster relief (interview 44, October 30, 2014). The U.S. government pledged $87 million in disaster relief.

### Continuation of the Joint Special Operations Task Force—Philippines Transition

Despite the Zamboanga siege and the typhoon, JSOTF-P continued to move forward with transition. During Colonel Beaudette's command, he reduced the JSOTF-P footprint to 300 and then developed a transition plan to reduce personnel to 100. The footprint shrank to a company-sized element in Zamboanga, an MSOT in Jolo, and an ODA in Cotabato.

By October 2014, the JSOTF-P HQ's primary subordinate element was TF South, led by an NSW PLT. By year's end, the element had transitioned to Team South, an ODA with a CA and MIST. All out-stations were closed except Camp Navarro, but warm bases were maintained on Basilan and Jolo for expeditionary advisers. Two MSOT marines remained on Jolo, and six Navy SEALs remained on Basilan as LCEs (interview 19, October 6, 2014). TF North, a company element, was replaced by Team North. As part of the transition plan, the PAT assumed oversight of Team North and LCE elements based in Manila and Aguinaldo.

The focus of advisory efforts continued to be institutional-level engagement and preparation for Phase 0 transition. Colonel McDowell spent five days in Manila and two in Zamboanga. Time in Manila was devoted to working with the PAT and country team to build relationships that would allow for a successful Phase 0 transition.

The initial timeline called for transition to Phase V by May 2014 and to Phase 0 by May 2015. Colonel McDowell proposed the creation of the Joint Intelligence Task Force—Mindanao (JITF-M) to facilitate intelligence-sharing and analysis among all the security forces in Mindanao (interview 44, September 30, 2014). The JITF-M, located at Camp Navarro, was intended to support both WestMinCom and EastMinCom, as well as the assigned police forces and intelligence agencies. JSOTF-P provided extensive training to its members on intelligence collection and analysis, as well as organizational and advisory support. Several interviewees observed the reluctance of individual commands and services to share intelligence and that the JITF-M would not likely progress without sustained support from the United States.

As the transition proceeded, the U.S. embassy shared some of the JSOTF-P concerns about the loss of valuable capabilities. The embassy sent a cable to Washington stressing the importance of maintaining some SOF capability and cautioning against withdrawing JSOTF-P too quickly (interview 26, October 7, 2014). The embassy recognized that it would be difficult to replace the long-standing ties that JSOTF-P had developed with most local government officials from the provincial to the barangay levels in Mindanao, Basilan, and Sulu. It was also reliant on JSOTF-P for force protection and transport to outlying areas not served by commercial flights (interview 26, October 7, 2014). Finally, with JSOTF-P's departure, many development and outreach programs would end. USAID would not be able to reach many remote areas without JSOTF-P's protection and transport.

### Hedging the Risks to Transition

As likely the last JSOTF-P commander, Colonel Brown sought to minimize the risks created by JSOTF-P's closure. His assessment concluded that JSOTF-P's departure would create higher operational risk and a gap in situational awareness. To mitigate that risk, he proposed several measures to maintain situational awareness and prevent backsliding in the southern Philippines, including

- maintaining a small presence in the south
- strengthening relationships with both PSF and U.S. interagency partners via regular key-leader engagements
- embedding personnel in operations centers
- continuing aviation support for these activities
- continued intelligence-sharing and increased transparency in operations and activities (interview 19, October 6, 2014).

Under his plan, JSOTF-P activities would consist of 90 percent security-force assistance and only 10 percent operational advise and assist to support USPACOM CT objectives (interview 19, October 6, 2014). But, with his proposed adjustments, this model would be more robust than simply reverting to traditional Phase 0 security cooperation activities consisting of episodic training and exercises. It was, in his view, critical to undertake activities that would permit U.S. forces to maintain awareness of PSF operations and any changes in the threat environment. Informed by his assessment, SOCPAC approved the extension of mobility assets for JSOTF-P into 2015.

A significant wild card for the southern Philippines was the CAB; its implementation was slated to occur after approval by the legislature and a subsequent plebiscite, at about the same time as JSOTF-P disbanded. The accord, promising greater autonomy for a larger area of the southern Philippines, could affect the security situation in a variety of ways. The new government might reduce targeting toward Islamic extremist organizations, unrest might be renewed if the agreement failed to be implemented, or the new Bangsamoro security forces might prove unable to provide adequate security. In addition, MILF members might refuse to disarm and instead flock to the Muslim extremist groups (interview 33, October 10, 2014).

One of the central concerns as JSOTF-P contemplated the future was to avoid "backsliding" or a renewal of the threat and retrograde in PSF capability. Although the transnational terrorist threat was generally considered to be degraded across the southern Philippines, it was not defeated. In the judgment of one commander, the threat is not as diminished as it should be after the investments made in the past decade plus (interview 19, October 6, 2014). The shadow of the U.S. withdrawal from Iraq also weighed on the command.

Specifically, the emergence of the Islamic State of Iraq and the Levant (ISIL) as a threat with potential global appeal and reach caused some speculation regarding the possibility of a resurgent threat of extremist violence in the southern Philippines. In July and August 2014, the ASG and BIFF (a splinter group of the MILF) both released videos declaring their support for ISIL, but Lt. Gen. Rustico O. Guerrero stated that there was no indication of a "direct linkage" between the groups and ISIL ("BIFF," 2014; Guerrero quoted in Alipala, 2014a). The general consensus expressed in formal assessments and interviews characterized the ASG as a criminal entity that views ransom and other revenue largely to sustain itself (interviews 2–4, 6, 8, 15, 22, 26, 33–38, and 44 with serving JSOTF-P and SOCPAC personnel and senior U.S. and Philippine officials interviewed in late 2014). However, intelligence analysts pointed out that continued collection and analysis would be required to detect any change in its intent or capability (interview 15, October 3, 2014; interview 33, October 10, 2014; interview 38, October 11, 2014). Advocating such continued vigilance, one interviewee noted that the ASG is "one leader away" from resuming an ideological mission (interview 34, October 10, 2014).

### Transition to Embassy Lead

The U.S. country team became the locus of activities previously shared in part by JSOTF-P. The Mindanao Working Group continued to function as the U.S. embassy's primary mechanism to coordinate all U.S. activities concerning Mindanao (Holt, 2011). The monthly meeting provided information on the region and updates on ongoing activities and identified future needs and opportunities for collaboration. The U.S. embassy also instituted or refined other coordination mechanisms. The Law Enforcement Working Group became the Rule of Law Committee, led by LEGAT, which recommends changes to GRP national laws, enabling a more effective CT campaign, and the International Criminal Investigative Training Assistance Program, led by the U.S. Department of Justice and the Federal Bureau of Investigation, which trains PSF law enforcement officers in investigative and forensic skills. Additional groups shared intelligence and coordinated informational activities through the public diplomacy and public affairs office, while the JUSMAG retained leadership of overall U.S.-GRP military-to-military relations.

USAID planned to continue much of its programming in the south, but the loss of JSOTF-P security and transport required some revision of its plans. USAID contracted with local nationals to provide security and transport, and increased its reliance on the AFP and PNP for personnel security and transportation. In the absence of JSOTF-P lift to Basilan and Jolo, however, U.S. civilian officials expected that the ability of USAID representatives to visit those areas would diminish and thus require an adjustment in their programming and execution (interview 23, October 7, 2014; interviews 24 and 26, October 7, 2014). As JSOTF-P drew down, USAID assumed responsibility for the Southern Philippines Public Perception Survey in order to maintain this valuable source of current information.

The relationship between JSOTF-P and JUSMAG fluctuated over time. Placing the deputy commander of JSOTF-P in Manila provided an ongoing mechanism to ensure close coordination with JUSMAG (interview 56, November 12, 2014). Some JSOTF-P personnel noted that, in later years, they increasingly operated at the operational and strategic levels to support national-level planning and coordination, as well as institutional development (interview 62, October 31, 2014). The two entities were charged with different missions that sometimes overlapped, and this created some tensions with two O-6s working at the same level (interview 27, October 7, 2014).

The impending transition required JSOTF-P and SOCPAC to navigate numerous bureaucratic, legal, and operational issues surrounding the future relationship of SOF to the U.S. embassy. The PAT would be responsible for SOF's enduring activities as the central remaining SOF node based at the embassy. With the end of a named operation and the consequent end of the JOA, the PAT and its personnel would operate under different authorities and funding than JSOTF-P had employed in its JOA under DoD-issued OEF-P authorities (interview 26, October 7, 2014; interview 27, October 7, 2014). In addition, future SOF personnel would be either on temporary duty (TDY) in the Philippines or assigned to the embassy as members of the country team. In the latter case, personnel would report to the senior defense officer (SDO). The embassy strongly preferred the latter arrangement to establish a clear line of authority and for practical reasons; TDY personnel are not assigned space and do not pay for it. The embassy was not prepared to support a large number of TDY personnel who arrive for four to six months and then extend their stays indefinitely. A large PAT would likely include both types of personnel.

The chain of command remained to be resolved, but, at minimum, the PAT would likely report to the embassy's SDO, as well as SOCPAC. The embassy's SDO, currently the O-6 JUSMAG chief, would become the supervisor rather than a colleague and peer. The JSOTF-P commanders typically informed JUSMAG of all their meetings and briefed him closely on relevant events, as a well-advised courtesy but not a formal requirement. Starting with the deference that Wurster and Fridovich had shown to the prerogatives of the U.S. ambassador, OEF-P had achieved and sustained a remarkable degree of coordination and synergy between the two entities' distinct but related missions in the service of U.S. security objectives in the Philippines. Given the long and proud history of JUSMAG in the Philippines (established in 1947, with a staff of 300 led by a major general), a PAT larger than JUSMAG's 24-person staff could cause tension if not properly designed and managed (interview 27, October 7, 2014).

As the transition progressed, the PAT grew from three people in 2013 to 25 in 2014. The planned size was about 50, divided between Manila and the JITF-M at Zamboanga. While assuming oversight and new roles, the PAT would continue its previous role, gathering and sharing terrorism-related information with the 17 other organizations in the Philippines. The PAT's twin roles would be to provide CT analysis and to orchestrate the ongoing advisory assistance and institutional support provided principally to Philippine SOF partners. With the departure of the relatively robust JSOTF-P capacity, the PAT expected to increasingly rely on interagency collaboration, particularly for intelligence (interview 27, October 7, 2014).

In accordance with U.S. policy guidance and U.S. military orders, the transition to steady-state operations was to be complete by the end of FY 2015, or September 30, 2015. JSOTF-P conducted a gradual turnover of functions to the PAT and deactivated on February 24, 2015.

## Summary

Between 2012 and 2014, JSOTF-P prepared for an end to OEF-P and the continuation of security activities under civilian authority with reduced U.S. personnel. Two events—an uprising and hostage crisis and then a major typhoon—slowed the transition. The first event, in September 2013, demonstrated the PSF's ability to conduct complex crisis operations in a dense and fragile urban environment. It highlighted the high degree of competence achieved by Philippine SOF in particular, as well as the progress made by the newer police SAF.

Neither the Philippine government nor the U.S. government sought a hasty transition that might jeopardize the gains in reducing the threat and increasing capabilities over the past 12 years. JSOTF-P gradually reduced its staff while maintaining a distributed footprint that would provide situational awareness and continuing support as required to PSF partners.

During this period, JSOTF-P continued its emphasis on institutional development and operational HQ support. It provided the needed support for creation of JITF-M in Zamboanga, supplying training, advice, and equipment to foster intelligence-sharing and analysis among all the Philippine commands. JSOTF-P envisioned JITF-M as an enduring structure for Philippine intelligence fusion and a node where U.S. SOF could plug in to maintain continued visibility as needed. It would ideally enable both Philippine and U.S. forces to gain an early warning of any resurgent transnational threat. Initial operations were moderately successful, but U.S. SOF interviewees noted that units from different commands and services remained somewhat reluctant to share intelligence.

As JSOTF-P decreased its staff, it transferred responsibilities to the PAT at the U.S. embassy, assisting its manning and capabilities to ensure that it could perform needed ongoing functions. As a result of the JSOTF-P final assessment, a more gradual transition was implemented with increased contacts, continued mobility, and additional operational advisory activities to mitigate the risk that threats might increase in the south or the AFP's response might falter.

In preparation for the transition, JSOTF-P and the PAT assisted the embassy country team to mitigate the loss of lift, force protection, situational awareness, and monitoring of U.S. civilian programs in the south, particularly in economic development and law enforcement. With the departure of JSOTF-P intelligence assets, a greater premium would be placed on increased interagency collaboration and sharing. Finally, the JSOTF-P worked with USPACOM and the embassy to coordinate future episodic training, advise-and-assist programs, other security cooperation activities, and security assistance programs to support further development of PSF capabilities. Through these measures, JSOTF-P sought to ensure a successful conclusion to OEF-P.

### Western Mindanao Command Assessment

Under General Guerrero, WestMinCom conducted a comprehensive assessment of the AFP campaign in the southern Philippines in 2014 (Headquarters, WestMinCom, undated). The document outlines the command's campaign plan against the multiple threat groups and evaluates progress through detailed measures of performance, as well as measures of effectiveness. WestMinCom is directed by its higher HQ and policy to pursue three distinct objectives in regard to the multiple threat groups: to defeat the ASG, to push the communist NPA (the Western Mindanao Regional Party Committee) back to negotiations, and to support the government peace process with the MILF (interview 35, October 10, 2014). To achieve those objectives, WestMinCom conducts a range of lethal and especially nonlethal operations, such as information support affairs, CA, and public affairs. The command's mission also includes enabling law enforcement to assume more responsibility per the IPSP: to "support law enforcement operations of different Law Enforcement Agencies in order to help the people within AOR create an environment conducive for sustainable development and a just and lasting peace."

The WestMinCom assessment characterized the state of campaign and specified the further actions the command intended to take, as summarized below:

- **ASG:** Not completely isolated. They still enjoy freedom of movement and links with other threat groups and key personalities in local government. Recommendations include revisiting strategies; concepts; and tactics, techniques, and procedures to defeat the ASG; initiating interagency collaboration to achieve unified actions in addressing the ASG; and effectively collaborating with the MILF and MNLF (Basilan) to further isolate the ASG in Basilan.
- **Western Mindanao Regional Party Committee:** Lack of a comprehensive approach to area clearing and dismantling guerrilla fronts, misidentification of center of gravity because of faulty mission analysis, and failure of joint mechanisms to coordinate and operate together. Recommendations include a comprehensive approach to clear provinces and guerrilla fronts, conducting deliberate mission analysis focusing on determining the center of gravity, and transforming the joint mechanism from a coordination mechanism into a platform for interagency and joint operations.
- **MILF:** Lack of a contingency plan in case the peace process fails, and no policy guidance after signing the CAB to address potentially contentious issues. Recommendations include maintaining strong adherence to the peace process and developing a contingency plan in case the peace process fails.
- **BIFF:** Lack of formal declaration calling BIFF a law enforcement problem or a threat to national security, compromise when seek-

ing clearance through a cease-fire, and high reliance on local government units and other security agencies to address BIFF issues. Recommendations include intensifying efforts to further isolate the BIFF from the MILF and strengthen local government unit and PNP ability to counter BIFF and address peace and security.

- **Rogue MNLF elements:** Diminished popular support because of the Zamboanga siege, with 527 casualties and factionalism within the organization. Recommendations include continuing to monitor the activities to preclude any unforeseen atrocities.

CHAPTER EIGHT

# Conclusion

This concluding chapter's primary purpose is to evaluate the overall effect of U.S. special operations in OEF-P, which directed U.S. SOF to support the PSF in countering transnational terrorist threats in the southern Philippines. The mission was conducted under terms of reference and ROE that prohibited a U.S. combat role but permitted a wide array of U.S. special operations activities in support of Philippine security operations and institutional development. OEF-P constitutes an important case study in the robust and extended application of U.S. special operations capabilities in support of another country's forces.

We used historical research methods, primarily interviews with participants and exploitation of primary source documents, to construct an authoritative narrative account of the principal activities and outcomes of OEF-P. We developed an evaluative framework to assess the outcomes in terms of effect on the transnational threat group and its support among the population, as well as the PSF's capabilities at the tactical, operational, and institutional levels. Because the formal command assessments and most of the official records remain unavailable to the public, the evidence adduced in support of the findings consists of three quantitative measures and interviews from multiple sources, supported by documentation.

The preceding chapters concluded with partial outcomes achieved during a given time period of the U.S. SOTF's 2002–2014 existence in terms of (1) the threat and threat conditions in the southern Philippines and (2) development of PSF capabilities. As these chapters illustrate, progress was neither linear nor complete: Threats moved, evolved, and continued to derive strength from underlying conditions, including the presence of conflict drivers and other threat groups. However, the transnational terrorist character of the armed activity did diminish substantially during the period studied.

An important caveat must be noted. U.S. SOF activities were not carried out in a vacuum. Much of USAID's programming and funds, for example, were devoted to the southern Philippines. The JSOTF-P inputs were the most-sustained and -intensive external inputs specifically oriented to security objectives during the period studied. JSOTF-P provided an average of 500 to 600 troops equipped with a wide array of enablers, including air, sea, and land mobility platforms, ISR assets, and medical personnel. These personnel were constantly present and engaged at all echelons with a wide variety of Philippine partners, and the great majority of them served multiple tours, which created a base of knowledge and relationships that further increased their impact. The effort entailed an estimated investment of $52 million annually, according to one source, considerably less than the tens of billions spent each year in Iraq and Afghanistan (Boot and Bennet, 2009).[1] Furthermore, JSOTF-P was the only enduring non-Philippine presence in the south. By contrast, all other external partners' engagement in the south was episodic or via an implementing partner. The TF made a concerted effort to coordinate its own efforts with those of other U.S. government entities to increase synergy and reduce redundancy. These factors all indicate that a significant effect could be expected from U.S. SOF inputs.

The inputs provided by other U.S. government activities also contributed to effects achieved, though this report does not attempt to assess their relative impact. The principal inputs included a large development program by USAID in Mindanao, a conflict-resolution effort until 2006, police training by other U.S. agencies, and annual exercises and training events organized and managed by the U.S. embassy's JUSMAG. The latter included both conventional forces assigned to USPACOM and a large number of JCET visits by U.S. SOF. The

---

[1] Overall U.S. military and economic assistance to the Philippines is approximately $200 million annually.

JCETs were oriented to improving Philippine special operations capability, so they constituted an effective episodic complement to the ongoing work of the SOTF.

Finally, the U.S. inputs of all types must be considered as complements to Philippine inputs. The Philippine government undertook significant efforts to improve its security forces and to bring peace and stability to the southern Philippines. These inputs included the IPSP, negotiations issuing in a new peace accord, reintegration and development programs, and significant acquisitions of materiel to improve the capability of the security forces. Most significant from the security perspective is the fact that the PSF supplied the manpower and designed and executed all security operations.

The threat groups themselves provided another set of inputs. The transnational threats ASG and JI demonstrated resilience, mobility, and the continued ability to sustain their operations through criminal activities and some degree of external support. The archipelago environment provided them natural advantages in terms of sanctuary. They shifted location and level of activity throughout the time period, eluding capture and maintaining the ability to conduct operations. Both the transnational groups and the MILF and MNLF armed militants aided each other and provided synergy and mutual support through cooperation, sanctuary, and recruitment. The groups depended on support from specific towns and other geographic areas and clan and family networks. All of these advantages dwindled slowly during the 14 years studied, on Basilan, Sulu, and Mindanao. The groups are not eradicated, but their notable decline in activity and freedom of movement suggests that the U.S. SOF efforts, combined with the GRP and AFP efforts, produced this result. The persistent activity of the threat groups suggests that, with the exception of those who demobilized, they did not unilaterally cease or diminish their operations. Another impetus to their continued activity is the degree to which corruption and political opportunism support armed action.

Given the large and varied number of inputs, it cannot be claimed that the U.S. SOF effort in OEF-P achieved any outcomes singlehandedly. As a major input and the only ongoing, continuous U.S. effort physically present in southern Philippines between 2002 and 2014, however, the U.S. SOF effort can be reasonably posited as a substantial contributor to the effects achieved. The following summary lists the outcomes and the evidence for them, the principal contributing factors, and the principal limiting factors that impeded greater effects.

## Overall Outcomes

### Reduced Transnational Terrorist Threat and Threat Conditions

With U.S. assistance, AFP forces disrupted enemy operations, denied safe haven, and controlled key terrain; AFP SOF conducted surgical operations against numerous key targets, facilitators, and resources. In the course of OEF-P, the transnational terrorist threat migrated from Basilan to Mindanao, to Jolo, and back to Mindanao and Basilan. Sanctuary and support for the ASG and JI were diminished after CMO, combat operations, and conflict-resolution efforts of the Philippine government.

Three types of evidence support this finding that the transnational terrorist threat in the Philippines has been significantly reduced during OEF-P: (1) a decline in enemy-initiated attacks, (2) reductions in the number of members of the ASG, and (3) poll data showing decreased support for the ASG and increased satisfaction with government security forces. This change in the population's sentiment correlates with the increased intensity of CMO and IO. The poll data support heat maps that show the ASG's diminished freedom of movement in areas where the ASG and related JI elements operated in the southern Philippines.[2] The detailed data follow:

- According to data collected by the ESOC project for the Philippines, enemy-initiated attacks in the ASG's three primary areas of operation, Basilan, Sulu, and Tawi-Tawi, declined 56 percent between 2000 and 2012 (ESOC, undated). The attack-rate decline was not linear, and southern Basilan continues to be an

[2] Many of our interviewees (e.g., 26, 52, and 53) cited these heat maps, but the actual maps are not available to the public.

area of unrest. Figure 8.1 depicts the attack-rate trends in Basilan, Sulu, and Tawi-Tawi provinces.

- The number of ASG-armed militants declined from an estimated 1,270 to 437 members, according to the AFP. The U.S. State Department annual report estimated that the ASG declined from more than 2,200 to 400 armed members.[3]
- Independent polls show increased support for the security forces and decreased support for the ASG by a large majority of the population in areas where the ASG was most active. In 2011, U.S. SOF contracted an independent polling firm to assess public opinion in six "conflict-affected areas" of the Mindanao region; this Southern Philippines Public Perception Survey found that the number of those who reported being satisfied with the Philippine security services increased from 51 percent in 2011 to 63 percent in 2014. Over the same time period, the number of those expressing trust in the ASG declined from 8 percent to 2.5 percent (Teutsch and Thambidurai, 2014, pp. 59, 74).[4] The same polling firm conducted focus groups and reported that residents were open to increased U.S. presence because of the benefits they perceived from the U.S. SOF presence, including improved security forces, medical care, and infrastructure.

These polling and focus-group data, together with the reported reduction in enemy freedom of movement as shown by the heat maps, suggest that the intensive CMO undertaken by U.S. SOF and AFP achieved both the tactical objectives of securing access and information from the population and some strategic impact of denying support and resources to the ASG and increased support for the GRP. To the

---

[3] Headquarters, WestMinCom, undated, cites statistics through mid-2014. Other sources cite lower numbers of ASG militants as of 2014. For example, "Country Reports on Terrorism 2013" (U.S. Department of State, 2014) estimated the number of ASG members at 400. The department's 2000 report, *Patterns of Global Terrorism*, estimated the number of ASG members at "more than 2,000" (U.S. Department of State, 2001). The Associated Press put the number of ASG even lower, at 300 (Gomez, 2014).

[4] In addition, 86 percent of respondents said that the AFP was making their area safer, and 79 percent said that the PNP were making their area safer (pp. 42, 36).

degree that this is correct, these outcomes serve as the primary bulwark to prevent the decreased attack levels and decreased threat groups from growing again. Diffusion and temporary suppression are common occurrences in guerrilla warfare, and only residents' permanent and active rejection of sanctuary, support, and resources will insure against a return or resurgence of the threat in these areas. Figure 8.1 shows the decline in attacks by the group over the past decade in each province of primary activity (Tawi-Tawi served primarily as a transit zone and haven).

Progress in reducing the transnational terrorist threat over the course of OEF-P was neither linear nor complete. The "balloon effect" could be observed as the locus of the threat and high-value individuals moved from one island to another, as Figure 8.1 indicates. Consistent application of sound counterinsurgency practices that denied the enemy the support of the population (and rival armed groups), resources, and sanctuaries gradually increased the effectiveness of AFP operations and shrank the threat groups' room for maneuver. However,

**Figure 8.1**
**Enemy-Initiated Attacks, by Province and Year**

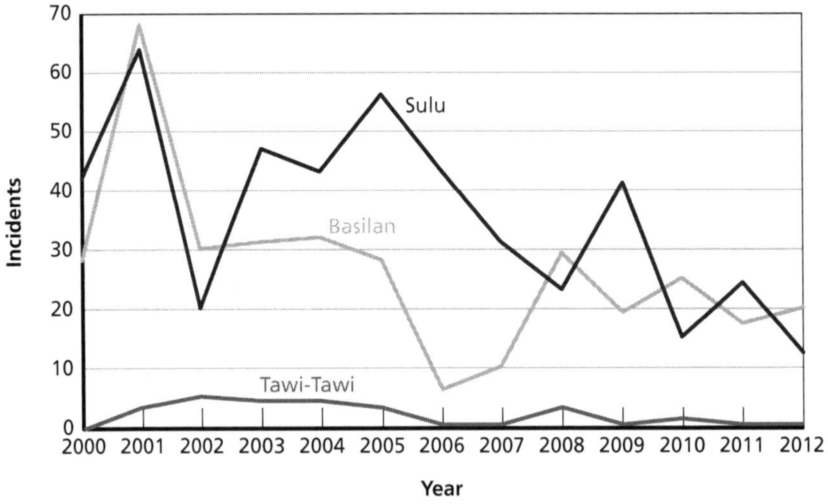


SOURCE: ESOC data.
RAND *RR1236-8.1*

both Philippine and U.S. officers interviewed believed that a resurgent terrorist threat is possible and that continued vigilance and application of sound counterinsurgency practices are warranted.

As of 2015, both the U.S. and Philippine military commands characterized the transnational terrorist threat as having been reduced to a largely criminal phenomenon, although some of the terrorist leaders remain at large. The geography of the Philippines continues to provide a potential sanctuary and training ground for a possibly resurgent threat from Malaysia or Indonesia, and some interviewees noted that groups have voiced support for ISIL. Philippine and U.S. commanders and intelligence officers recommended continued vigilance to guard against the possibility that a new ideological leader might surface to regenerate violent extremist organizations (interview 34, October 10, 2014; interview 33, October 10, 2014; interview 15, October 3, 2014; interview 26, October 7, 2014). Pledges of fealty to ISIL made by the ASG and BIFF signal such a possibility. However, the death of a key JI leader in the Philippines in a costly January 2015 operation might have reduced the operational linkages to transnational terrorist groups.

### Increased Philippine Security Forces Capabilities

Between 2001 and 2014, the PSF increased their capabilities at the (1) tactical, (2) operational, and (3) institutional levels, albeit to differing degrees. The primary evidence supporting this finding is assessments by U.S. and Philippine military officers whom we interviewed, along with official documentation. Both U.S. and Philippine interviews support the detailed findings below. On the whole, civilian interviewees, including former U.S. ambassadors, senior Philippine civilian officials, and veteran journalist Maria A. Ressa, agreed with the U.S. and Philippine military interviewees' judgment that PSF capabilities had increased dramatically during those 14 years. U.S. SOF contributed to this increased capability by providing training, advice, assistance, and some equipment. However, numerous U.S. SOF interviewees also noted that leaks continue to compromise military operations and that numerous local political actors used the ongoing conflict to their benefit. In addition, one former JSOTF-P commander believed that the PSF capabilities should have advanced further given the magnitude and duration of U.S. support provided. Other U.S. SOF, particularly senior NCOs who have served five years or more in the Philippines at regular intervals between 2001 and 2014, charted slow but steady progress in security force capabilities. A detailed summary of U.S. SOF contribution to capabilities developed at the tactical, operational, and institutional levels follows.

At the tactical level, U.S. SOF provided training, advice, and assistance to conventional Philippine Army, Marine Corps, Navy, and Air Force units at all echelons throughout Mindanao. In the later years of OEF-P, U.S. SOF also trained, advised, and assisted several BNs of the PNP SAF. U.S. SOF provided intensive training, advice, and assistance, as well as equipment, to the Philippine SOF, particularly the LRR and, to a lesser degree, the NAVSOG, the Scout Rangers, and the SF. Most U.S. interviewees considered the Philippine special operations units to be the most tactically proficient elements of the AFP. One empirical analysis of operations in the mid-2000s found that Philippine SOF achieved higher enemy-casualty rates with lower civilian and friendly casualties than Philippine conventional forces (Felter, 2009). Two senior U.S. SOF interviewees judged that Philippine SOF are among the most proficient of those Asian SOF units with which they had worked (interview 41, October 11, 2014; interview 42, September 30, 2014).

AFP SOF units are generally viewed as very capable, with JSOG being the most elite of those. The JSOG HQ, as well as the LRR companies that supply half its manpower, has received the most-intensive training, advising, and equipping by U.S. SOF during the past 14 years, so it would stand to reason that its are the most-competent forces. The support U.S. SOF has provided to NAVSOG has been less extensive and intensive, but, in recent years, NSW has provided support at NAVSOG's Cavite headquarters, as well as to elements deployed in the south. The two older SOF units, the SRR and the SFR, have, to some degree, benefited from training and field advisory assistance from U.S. SOF; these units have also provided the recruits for the LRR's expansion. President Aquino ordered the LRR to be doubled in size from three to six LRCs (interview 30, October 9, 2014; interview 35, October 10, 2014). The government also purchased additional arms and other equipment to support the expansion, although some military leaders interviewed advocate filling out the current three Light Reaction Battalions, which are understrength by approximately half.

At the operational level, U.S. SOF advised and assisted various AFP HQ to improve their joint processes and integrate C2, planning, and intelligence functions. U.S. SOF assisted and provided equipment for WestMinCom to establish a joint operations center and lower-echelon fusion centers that included police and to improve the integration of air–ground operations. These advisory functions extended to WestMinCom's lower echelons, including JTF Comet and division and BDE staffs. U.S. SOF also provided intensive advice and assistance in the creation of JSOG and operational HQ.

At the operational level, JSOTF-P devoted particular attention to improving conventional and SOF integration and the appropriate employment of SOF by AFP commands. AFP SOF elements have historically been commanded and controlled by conventional commanders, and many interviewees agreed that some of these commanders did not understand how to use SOF, so they were used incorrectly (interview 48, November 6, 2014). It was only in recent years that Philippine SOF units began fully participating in joint operations with conventional units and that their elite training capabilities have been employed correctly on a regular basis (for example, interview 19, October 6, 2014). The newly developed SOF operational commands will be employed, most interviewees agreed, under the JTF commander if not a lower echelon.

At the institutional level, U.S. SOF contributed somewhat to strategy, planning, and coordination at the AFP national HQ, and they helped WestMinCom develop its plans and intelligence analysis and fusion capabilities. WestMinCom's 2014 campaign assessment illustrates an advanced ability to conduct planning and assessment. This assessment evaluates the campaign's progress in detailed fashion using measures of performance and measures of effectiveness to assess the progress achieved and the shortcomings across the lines of effort. The assessment recommended specific steps to improve joint and interagency unity of effort, improved maritime interdiction capability, and collaboration with recently demobilized threat groups to further isolate the ASG. In response to one of the findings, WestMinCom also formed a JTF to address the C2 issues across the JOA, which was an important step to adapt to JSOTF-P's withdrawal and the seams between efforts on Basilan, Sulu, and Tawi-Tawi (Headquarters, WestMinCom, undated).

U.S. SOF assisted most intensively in the institutional development of Philippine SOF force-providing HQ, including SOCOM PA, the Army SOF HQ, and the institutions and processes to create a self-sustaining SOF enterprise. With U.S. SOF assistance, Philippine SOF developed a training cadre, schoolhouse, selection criteria, courses, doctrine, and an NCO academy. For many years, this has been a self-sustaining capability. Most recently, U.S. SOF assisted in the standardization of programs of instruction across the various SOF units.

One of the most-significant and enduring impacts of JSOTF-P's relationship with the AFP was the latter's adoption of intensive CMO as a principal pillar of its approach to the southern Philippines and its institutionalization of a CMO capability. The AFP formally adopted the "80/20" principle of the desired proportion of CMO to kinetic operations and showed early results in Basilan as a means to gain population support and reduce the enemy room for maneuver and sanctuary (Lambert, Lewis, and Sewall, 2012, pp. 123–124).

The shift began in April 2007 under then–AFP chief of staff General Hermogenes C. Esperon, Jr., and was applied by successive commanders of JTF Comet in the southern Philippines. Several Philippine generals described the shift away from a highly kinetic approach on Jolo island, the scene of long-running high-intensity fighting (interview 22, October 7, 2014; interviews 35 and 36, October 10, 2014). A key MILF leader declared that the AFP CMO activities were "more lethal than brute force" ("Partnered Counterterrorism Operations in the Philippines," 2011). A majority of U.S. and Philippine interviewees noted this enthusiastic embrace of CMO. In addition, the AFP took several steps to institutionalize a CMO capability, creating a command and manning it with organic and assigned units. In the later years of OEF-P, U.S. SOF personnel supported this institutional development by contributing to programs of instruction, doctrinal manuals, and development of subject-matter expertise.

The U.S. and Philippine military interviewees agreed that PSF capabilities had improved from 2001 to 2014. Battlefield results from 2001 to 2014 support the assertion that the AFP have become more capable of planning and executing complex joint operations, resupplying their forces, evacuating their casualties, and minimizing collateral damage and displacement of civilians. Maritime interdiction operations have improved somewhat, and the PAF has acquired some degree of proficiency in night vision–enabled operations, precision close air support, FWD air control, and air–ground integration.

Although it is possible that the PSF would have developed these capabilities without U.S. SOF's assistance, current and former AFP officers who served at various echelons of conventional and special operations units stated that U.S. SOF contributed significantly to increased proficiency of their command staffs and leaders in such areas as fusing intelligence and operations and planning and executing complex operations. They stated that the training, advice, intelligence, and equipment that U.S. SOF provided to the PSF had increased their capabilities and troops' confidence and lowered casualty and mortality rates.

Despite the improvements, significant gaps remain in joint operations because of rivalries among the military services and even more so in police–military coordination, as well as the overall proficiency and reputation of the PNP, which consistently ranks lower than the military in opinion polls conducted by the U.S. State Department.[5] U.S.-instituted fusion cells enhanced cooperation with the police in Mindanao, but frictions continued to impede police–military coordination in many instances, according to both U.S. and Philippine interviewees and the evidence of several operations, including the high-casualty January 2015 operation.[6] Furthermore, both U.S. and Philippine inter-

---

[5] Polls that the U.S. State Department's Office of Opinion Research gave us show a consistently higher level of confidence in the military than in the police. The average difference in confidence ratings of ten years of polls was 11.8 percent. In 2004, the last year for which poll results can be reported in a publication, 65 percent of respondents expressed "a great deal" or "a fair amount" of confidence in the armed forces, and 55 percent expressed "a great deal" or "a fair amount" of confidence in the police.

[6] During an ill-fated operation on January 24, 2015, 44 PNP SAF troops were ambushed and killed after a successful operation that killed the top JI target in the country, a Malaysian

viewees doubted that the PNP would be ready to assume responsibility nationwide for internal security by 2016, as called for in the Philippine IPSP.

### Enhanced U.S.-Philippine Relationship

The SOTF was charged with two specific objectives: (1) to support and improve the PSF's ability to counter terrorism and (2) in so doing, to reduce the transnational terrorist threat. Accomplishing this twofold mission incidentally contributed to another outcome, which was an enhanced bilateral relationship. The United States seeks to maintain access to the Philippines and to enhance its military-to-military ties, as well as the overall bilateral relationship. Several interviewees with national strategic experience stated that the conduct of the OEF-P mission, under terms that respected Philippine sovereignty and aided Philippine security objectives, contributed to these overarching U.S. national security objectives. One former U.S. ambassador noted that the southern Philippines continues to be an area of relative neglect and lesser strategic importance for the national government, so the contributions of OEF-P to the overall bilateral relationship should be placed in that context (interview 64, December 4, 2014). Other interviewees, including a U.S. ambassador and former AFP chief of staff, noted that both Presidents Arroyo and Aquino closely monitored the SOF efforts, and they and their senior leaders made several visits to the south (interview 65, December 15, 2014; interview 39, October 11, 2014). The Philippine military officer corps all served multiple tours in the south as their primary combat tours, and most senior military leaders retained positive views of U.S. SOF from their close interactions in the south. Several senior U.S. and Philippine officials believed that the extended and, on balance, very positive experience of OEF-P contributed to a renewal and deepening of U.S.-Philippine relations, which had been attenuated by the 1992 base closures and diminished U.S. aid (interview 65, December 15, 2014; interview 39, October 11, 2014; interview 59, November 3, 2014; interview 36, October 10, 2014;

---

facilitator known as Marwan. The deaths and ensuing national debate dimmed prospects for ratification of the terms of a peace agreement concluded with the MILF in 2014.

interview 66, November 17, 2014). Polls showed that Philippine public opinion remains highly favorable to the United States, among the most favorable view of the United States held in the world.[7] The signing of the Enhanced Defense Cooperation agreement in 2014, which permits more-extensive defense cooperation, including the presence of U.S. forces, signaled the Philippine government's desire for closer security cooperation in the future.

## Limiting Factors

*Tactical focus delayed institutional development and might have contributed to delayed transition.* Some interviewees lodged two critiques of an otherwise-successful mission that exemplified sound planning. First, the balance of effort for many years focused on tactical advisory and training activities rather than building staff processes at higher-level HQ and assisting institutional growth and sustainment. Second, many interviewees concurred with the formal assessment that the mission might have successfully transitioned some years earlier. In the later years, the SOTF placed increased emphasis on staff and institutional development, as well as operational-level advising, and left much of the training to cadres. The late development of higher-level processes might have contributed to the delayed transition, although numerous other factors were involved. Some additional factors that limited effectiveness in the early years included short JSOTF command tours that limited the continuity and influence of JSOTF-P, both with its GRP partners and within the U.S. embassy country team and uncertainty about the future trajectory of OEF-P, its scope, and the terms under which troops would operate. U.S. SOF leaders had expected that results would require a sustained, multiyear commitment, but the political sensitivities constituted an important impediment to long-term planning in the initial years.

---

[7] According to the Pew Research Center's spring 2014 Global Attitudes survey, 92 percent of Filipinos view the United States favorably (Pew Research Center, 2014).

*The security-force assistance efforts of the TF were insufficiently coordinated with security assistance and security cooperation activities.* Despite efforts to develop close coordination between the U.S. embassy and JSOTF-P, the exercises and security assistance for which the JUSMAG was responsible were not always aligned with JSOTF-P's security-force assistance to produce the maximum lasting increase in needed AFP capabilities. This gap between the two efforts left numerous institutional and capability needs unmet. An additional problem affected U.S. security assistance (i.e., hardware purchases and sales), according to some interviewees because the AFP sometimes purchased platforms, such as helicopters and planes, that were not the most appropriate for their needs. Regarding institutional development, JSOTF-P did possess the specialized knowledge to train the AFP on program management and certain staff functions at higher HQ. Ideally, this deficit would be addressed through security cooperation activities, and JSOTF-P recommended that USPACOM staff trainers be sent to the Philippines for this purpose (interview 19, October 6, 2014). Ongoing JCETs could also address some of the institutional training needs, but the timing and type of exercises would need to be carefully planned to enable a coordinated development of capability in critical areas.

*Gaps in AFP capability and capacity remain despite years of training and assistance.* Poor tactical skills on the part of conventional forces indicated that the AFP had no universally effective training methods for continuing to impart skill that U.S. SOF had taught to dozens of units in 14 years. As one officer noted, a poorly dressed wound caused the death of an infantryman in the fall of 2014, despite years of combat lifesaver training provided by the SOTF. At a higher level, operational results demonstrated increased competence by commanders in conducting complex operations that integrated joint forces, including maritime infiltration and close air support, and in executing speedy and effective evacuation of casualties. Senior leaders produce coherent and sophisticated strategies, plans, and assessments. However, a service-centric culture impedes joint operations, timely provision of forces and materiel, and intelligence-sharing. Material capacity and capability limitations continued to exist, particularly in terms of aircraft, although purchases have recently been made. The U.S. Air Force advisory element of JSOTF-P assessed that inappropriate platforms had been purchased, without the needed training and spare-parts packages (interviews 31 and 54, October 9 and 27, 2014). Finally, security leaks compromised numerous operations, suggesting, at minimum, a need for greater counterintelligence capability.[8]

*The drivers of conflict continue to exist in the south.* Despite the GRP's efforts to address the underlying drivers of conflict in the southern Philippines, most prominently through negotiated accords, the problems of poverty, discrimination, lack of basic services and economic opportunity, corruption, and criminality continue. The approval and enactment of the CAB represents an opportunity for successful demobilization, disarmament, and reintegration of many of the armed Muslim separatists. Further military and law enforcement action might be required to deal with the remnants of the ASG and splinter groups, as well as to push the NPA back to the negotiating table, but economic development in the area might be the best guarantor of long-term stability. As noted above, as long as these conditions remain, the renewed wave of global jihadism spurred by ISIL's dramatic rise in 2014 could ignite a resurgence of extremist violence in the southern Philippines.

## Key Contributing Factors

### Maintaining the Sovereign Lead Avoided U.S. Dependency

Perhaps the most important feature of the OEF-P mission was the heavy emphasis the United States placed on the Philippines' sovereignty, which defined the way in which the mission would be carried out—i.e., by the Philippine forces with U.S. forces in a supporting role. From the very beginning of U.S. involvement in 2001, U.S. leadership agreed that respecting Philippine sovereignty and its lead role in confronting terrorism there was the highest priority and that U.S. forces,

---

[8] Many U.S. SOF interviewees who had served multiple years in the southern Philippines suggested that local and family ties, corruption, and cultural acceptance of deal-making contributed to operational outcomes.

while remaining under their own chain of command, would support AFP priorities.

The ROE for U.S. SOF advisers included the ability to advise in the battlefield at BN and sometimes company command and to provide direct support, but advisers were to remain "one terrain feature away" from the adversary. Numerous U.S. SOF interviewees felt that more-restrictive rules early in OEF-P deprived U.S. SOF of influence, credibility, and visibility of Philippine capabilities. U.S. SOF were able to move forward with commanders into the battlefield under the later ROE, to advise and assist, although not to engage in combat (interview 72, August 14, 2013). The great majority of U.S. and Philippine interviewees embraced the ban on U.S. combat as essential to secure the necessary support among the Philippine government and public for the U.S. presence. As shown by the rejection of the proposed combat mission of JTF 555 in 2002 and 2003, Filipinos could tolerate and even embrace a robust advisory and support role for U.S. troops, but not a U.S. combat role.

In addition, maintaining Philippine forces in the lead ensured that the U.S. effort squarely focused on building and employing Philippine capability under Philippine-designed and -led operations. This avoided creating dependency on U.S. leadership, planning, and manpower and removed the need for an eventual transition to Philippine-led operations. For these reasons, the ROE prohibiting U.S. combat appear to have been warranted and, on the whole, beneficial in accomplishing the objectives of OEF-P. Other cases might dictate a different calculus (for example, a less capable partner or a more-lethal threat might warrant a direct combat advisory role for a time).

Regarding the prohibition on U.S. SOF providing operational assistance to PSF conducting operations against threats other than the transnational terrorist groups, that restriction also appeared to be amply warranted to comply with the GRP's preferred approach of negotiating with the Moro separatists. The collocation and some degree of cooperation among the armed threat groups made the U.S. SOF task more complex and difficult and ultimately placed a greater burden on WestMinCom to conduct its multipronged campaign plan. WestMinCom, it should be noted, carefully distinguished among the objectives prescribed for it regarding NPA, MILF and MNLF, and transnational terrorists. The NPA threat was not collocated and, in any case, not part of a transnational terrorist threat. In any event, the GRP was able to employ the improved PSF capabilities against the full range of threats.

### Assessment-Driven Plans and Operations

Assessments played a major role at key junctures of the OEF-P effort, informing the initial design of the plan, significant adaptations to the plan, and decisions to begin transitions to Phase V and Phase 0. This use of assessments helped ensure appropriate continuity of effort, as well as the needed adaptations. The major assessments spanned the strategic to tactical levels. Most JSOTF-P commanders conducted an initial assessment to refine the lines of effort according to current conditions and the progress of the effort. Tactical units also performed regular assessments of the population and environment to understand current conditions for planning current operations.

As discussed in Chapter Two, the TCAV provided a detailed initial assessment of the environment's enemy and human domains; it was designed to enable U.S. forces to use an indirect approach that would target the enemy by shrinking its room for maneuver among the population. The TCAV also set a precedent for close coordination by engaging both the U.S. embassy country team and the Philippine government in conducting the assessment jointly. This practice, in turn, solidified the relationships and sense of a shared mission that facilitated ongoing access.

As discussed in Chapter Three, SOCPAC conducted a strategic-, operational-, and tactical-level assessment of OEF-P in 2005. Using the TCAV assessment's methodology, the 2005 SOCPAC assessment found serious shortfalls in the population's access to services on Jolo island and increased threat activity throughout the Sulu archipelago; the assessment provided the basis for recommending that the population-centric CMO-heavy model used in Basilan be applied to the Sulu archipelago. Analysis of gaps in PSF capability led to expanded efforts to address them. An exception to the rule of assessments driving plan adaptation occurred in 2008, when the USPACOM assessment found that the objectives of OEF-P had been met and that transition could begin. This did not occur for several reasons, including the embassy's desire for continued JSOTF-P support in the south, as well as the TF's desire to realize gains from the ongoing effort to upgrade AFP close air support. The 2010 USPACOM assessment reconfirmed that conditions had been met for the conclusion of OEF-P and the withdrawal of JSOTF-P from the Philippines, and the process of planning and implementing the transition then began. Completion of the transition was delayed in part by the Zamboanga siege in 2013.

### Synergistic and Sustained Special Operations

The combined application of various special operations capabilities, with enablers, created a more powerful effect than might be expected of a force of 500 to 600 troops. OEF-P achieved considerable impact at all echelons, across all service branches, as well as SOF, in a wide variety of locations. CA units played a major role in the most prevalent line of operation, CMO, throughout the mission in every location, with a profound impact not only on the conflict but also on the Philippine approach to the conflict. MISTs also played significant roles in encouraging the population to assist in the efforts to end the violence perpetrated by the terrorist groups.

All four SOF service components (ARSOF, NSW, AFSOC, and U.S. Marine Corps Forces Special Operations Command) contributed personnel to improve and support Philippine ground, air, and maritime capabilities. Although the largest proportion of the force consisted of Army special operators, Navy SEALs also trained and advised both conventional and special counterparts in maritime operations and led a subordinate TF in much of the island environment. U.S. Air Force advisers trained Philippine airmen on a range of skills critical to air–ground integration and provided intelligence to support operations. Marine Corps SOF played a significant role in the later years of the effort. The TF operated throughout the JOA, a vast territory of islands, routinely splitting up teams to provide smaller advisory elements or even singletons to maximize their reach.

Although the ROE prohibited U.S. forces from engaging in combat (except as needed for self-defense), the wide range of roles that

U.S. forces did play to assist operations, as well as institutional development, is not widely understood. U.S. SOF provided advice from the JTF to the BN level and, at times, at the company level, including in the field. Because most BN commanders typically led from the front, U.S. SOF advisers were able to observe and advise at the FWD command posts. In later years, the advisory effort focused more on higher echelons at the unified command and at institutional HQ, with the aim of achieving longer-term effects by advising staffs on planning, doctrine, force generation, and other building blocks of the military profession.

The TF conducted intelligence collection, fusion, and analysis in support of Philippine operations through a host of ISR platforms and supporting elements. Joint operations centers and intelligence fusion cells were trained and equipped. In the field, the provision of ISR empowered the PSF and played a force-protection role for U.S. forces.

Other critical enablers included air and sea lift; medical care, including FWD surgical teams; and construction and engineering support. The U.S. Naval Construction Forces, also known as Seabees, and other engineering units built and improved roads (as well as piers and other structures) for the benefit of the population, as well as the prosecution of the military effort. Not only did sea, air, and land mobility platforms enable U.S. SOF to operate over wide distances, but, in emergencies, they were put at the service of the PSF to aid their operations. Although contract airlift was barred from hot landing zones, they extracted personnel from the nearest safe point. The combination of MEDEVAC, combat lifesaver training, and FWD surgical teams not only saved lives but created a wider benefit of increased confidence that encouraged the infantry to be more proactive. On occasion U.S. SOF violated the letter of their ROE to rescue wounded Philippine comrades. These acts of solidarity earned enormous gratitude and respect at all levels of the Philippine military.

### Interagency Cooperation

The JSOTF-P achieved a high level of coordination with the U.S. embassy country team over the 14 years of OEF-P. U.S. SOF and civilian officials disagreed at times over particular issues, but the strong leadership of four successive career ambassadors forged an effective civil–military partnership in this endeavor. In addition, the creation of structures such as the Mindanao Working Group provided enduring mechanisms for achieving whole-of-government synergy.

As discussed in Chapter Five, JSOTF-P's relationship with USAID grew and strengthened over the years. The placement of a JSOTF-P LNO at USAID's Manila office and a USAID LNO at JSOTF-P permitted increased collaboration in later years to reduce redundancy, increase effectiveness, and provide USAID a secure location in Mindanao. JSOTF-P provided "eyes and ears" to aid in monitoring and evaluation for many USAID projects, especially in more-remote and dangerous areas. USAID traveled to more places more often by dint of JSOTF-P air and maritime assets and security provided by the TF. In addition, as ambassadors and other members of the country team acknowledged, JSOTF-P directly supported U.S. country-team programs through providing force protection, mobility, and monitoring of projects that U.S. civilian officials would have been otherwise unable to visit (interview 24, October 7, 2014; interview 23, October 7, 2014; interview 64, December 4, 2014). Most of the U.S. military and civilian interviewees considered that the efforts made to create a synergistic interagency effort by both U.S. SOF and members of the country team exceeded those efforts made elsewhere, in their experiences.[9] However, interviewees also cited frictions that occurred at times over such issues as failure to tap the embassy's expertise, confer on country need assessments, agree on development priorities, and observe embassy guidance on public affairs, public diplomacy, or protocol matters.

## Generalizability of Findings

Although the scope of this study did not include testing the generalizability of these findings, they might apply to some degree to other cases

[9] An independent evaluation commissioned by USAID stated, "USAID and the Joint Special Operations Task Force—Philippines work closely together in several conflict areas of Mindanao to support the Philippine development objectives." See USAID, undated, pp. 4–5.

of long-duration special operations in countries with some capability and the political will to serve as the lead agent of security operations. The experience of U.S. SOF in the Philippines represents a positive return on a relatively small investment, as well as a possible model that could apply, to some degree, to other countries that seek assistance to address transnational or internal security threats, particularly where the United States cannot or will not deploy combat forces. Recent efforts in Colombia, Yemen, east and west Africa, and the Middle East offer points of comparison and contrast.

The level of threat and the nature, will, and capability of the government and its security forces are among the important variables determining the viability and chances of success of such efforts. In the case of the Philippines, despite a previous history of military rule, a more-recent incidence of coup attempts, some degree of anti-Americanism, corruption, and human-rights concerns, these negative factors were not severe enough to impede the outcomes achieved by sustained and multifaceted advisory and operational assistance and CMO of JSOTF-P in support of AFP operations in the south and the development of one of Asia's most-competent joint SOF (interview 42, September 30, 2014; interview 41, October 11, 2014).[10]

Some positive attributes also enhanced the prospects for success: The Philippine government has, in recent years, solidified its democratic rule, reduced the number of extrajudicial killings, and increased attention to socioeconomic and political drivers of conflict. It is considered a functioning, if flawed, democracy, ranked 69th out of 167 countries by the Economist Intelligence Unit (Lum and Dolven, 2014, p. 4). Some additional attributes that could limit the generalizability of the Philippine case include a long, historically close (if sometimes fraught) bilateral U.S. relationship. The Philippines having once been a U.S. colony, Americans and Filipinos are bound by a dense web of ties that includes 4 million Filipino Americans, a high proportion of English-

[10] These interviewees, who participated in training and advising of a half-dozen special operations units in Asia in the past 20 years, rated the Philippines just after Singapore's forces in overall competence. The concern over human-rights performance led the U.S. Congress to place a hold on a portion of U.S. assistance to the Philippine army, as noted in Lum and Dolven, 2014.

speaking Filipinos, and many Filipino officers who are graduates of the U.S. Military Academy at West Point (Lum and Dolven, 2014).

To ensure proper comparative frameworks, it must be emphasized that an essential feature of this case is the nature of the assistance provided: A sufficiently robust advisory force was authorized to provide *direct support to the partner's operations* in various locations, to multiple echelons and various security forces as the situation required. This operational assistance distinguishes such aid from security cooperation efforts or train-and-equip missions. Although U.S. SOF did not engage in combat, they did contribute directly to operations in many ways detailed here. Finally, the way in which U.S. SOF approached the OEF-P campaign could be its most important and fungible aspect—namely, the consistent application of principles of operational design and the synergistic application of varied special operations capabilities.[11]

---

[11] Appendix B provides a tool for the comparative evaluation of this and other cases' relevant features.

APPENDIX A

# Balikatan 02-1 Terms of Reference

On February 7, 2002, the Philippine Senate conducted a hearing on the Balikatan exercise, in which GRP vice president Teofisto T. Guingona, Jr., who was concurrently Secretary of Foreign Affairs, presented the draft terms of reference for Balikatan 02-1. Guingona's terms of reference were approved five days later. The approved terms of reference divided the GRP-U.S. agreement for Balikatan 02-1 into sections addressing two levels: the policy level and the exercise level. The approved terms of reference for Balikatan 02-1 are reproduced below.

I. POLICY LEVEL

1. The Exercise shall be Consistent with the Philippine Constitution and all its activities shall be in consonance with the laws of the land and the provisions of the [GRP]-US Visiting Forces Agreement (VFA).

2. The conduct of this training Exercise is in accordance with pertinent United Nations resolutions against global terrorism as understood by the respective parties.

3. No permanent US basing and support facilities shall be established. Temporary structures such as those for troop billeting, classroom instruction and messing may be set up for use by [GRP] and US Forces during the Exercise.

4. The Exercise shall be implemented jointly by [GRP] and US Exercise Co-Directors under the authority of the Chief

of Staff, AFP. In no instance will US Forces operate independently during field training exercises (FTX). AFP and US Unit Commanders will retain command over their respective forces under the overall authority of the Exercise Co-Directors. [GRP] and US participants shall comply with operational instructions of the AFP during the FTX.

5. The exercise shall be conducted and completed within a period of not more than six months, with the projected participation of 660 US personnel and 3,800 [GRP] Forces. The Chief of Staff, AFP shall direct the Exercise Co-Directors to wind up and terminate the Exercise and other activities within the six month Exercise period.

6. The Exercise is a mutual counter-terrorism advising, assisting and training Exercise relative to Philippine efforts against the ASG, and will be conducted on the Island of Basilan. Further advising, assisting and training exercises shall be conducted in Malagutay and the Zamboanga area. Related activities in Cebu will be for support of the Exercise.

7. Only 160 US Forces organized in 12-man Special Forces Teams shall be deployed with AFP field commanders. The US teams shall remain at the Battalion Headquarters and, when approved, Company Tactical headquarters where they can observe and assess the performance of the AFP Forces.

8. US exercise participants shall not engage in combat, without prejudice to their right of self-defense.

9. These terms of Reference are for purposes of this Exercise only and do not create additional legal obligations between the US Government and the Republic of the Philippines.

## II. EXERCISE LEVEL

### 1. TRAINING

a. The Exercise shall involve the conduct of mutual military assisting, advising and training of [GRP] and US Forces with the primary objective of enhancing the operational capabilities of both forces to combat terrorism.

b. At no time shall US Forces operate independently within [GRP] territory.

c. Flight plans of all aircraft involved in the exercise will comply with the local air traffic regulations.

### 2. ADMINISTRATION & LOGISTICS

a. [GRP] and US participants shall be given a country and area briefing at the start of the Exercise. This briefing shall acquaint US Forces on the culture and sensitivities of the Filipinos and the provisions of the VFA. The briefing shall also promote the full cooperation on the part of the [GRP] and US participants for the successful conduct of the Exercise.

b. [GRP] and US participating forces may share, in accordance with their respective laws and regulations, in the use of their resources, equipment and other assets. They will use their respective logistics channels.

c. Medical evaluation shall be jointly planned and executed utilizing [GRP] and US assets and resources.

d. Legal liaison officers from each respective party shall be appointed by the Exercise Directors.

3. PUBLIC AFFAIRS

a. Combined [GRP]-US Information Bureaus shall be established at the Exercise Directorate in Zamboanga City and at GHQ, AFP in Camp Aguinaldo, Quezon City.

b. Local media relations will be the concern of the AFP and all public affairs guidelines shall be jointly developed by [GRP] and US Forces.

c. Socio-Economic Assistance Projects shall be planned and executed jointly by [GRP] and US Forces in accordance with their respective laws and regulations, and in consultation with community and local government officials.[1]

---

[1] Quoted from *Lim v. Arroyo*, 2002.

APPENDIX B

# Plan Analysis Tool

The following questions are designed to assist in analysis of plan design, execution, assessment, and adaptation as performed by successive SOTFs over the course of OEF-P. This analytical tool can also be used to compare OEF-P with other cases of long-duration special operations. The intended use is for professional military education or as a reference guide for future policymaking, military planning, and operational design.

1. Plan design and adaptation. The mission statement for OEF-P directed U.S. SOF to counter transnational terrorist threats by supporting host-nation forces. The specific plan, lines of effort, and geographic focus evolved from 2002 to 2014; to what degree were these adaptations appropriate and effective?
2. Assessments. How were OEF-P assessments conducted by JSOTF-P and SOCPAC or USPACOM at various phases of the campaign? Were the assessments well conceived and useful in identifying the needed changes?
3. Resourcing the plan. What elements of the plan were well resourced, overresourced, or underresourced, and why? Was the right mix of special operations capabilities employed in sufficient numbers in the needed locations? What factors contributed to or detracted from continuity of effort across command iterations, including the way in which JSOTF-P HQ was manned?
4. Plan implementation. Did the noncombat ROE for U.S. SOF contribute to or prevent achievement of mission objectives?

5. Outcomes. Were the objectives achieved? Namely, did the security forces develop adequate capability to address the current level of threat? Was the stage set for successful steady-state operations with the appropriate footprint to continue intelligence and advisory assistance at the HQ level? What might have been done differently? Was the transition delayed unnecessarily; if so, what factors contributed to this delay? Was the effort too tactically focused at the expense of developing sustainable capability through force-provider institutions and the ability to employ it through higher-level operational JTF HQ? Were non-SOF security-force assistance efforts needed to address gaps; if so, would this have entailed a broader effort by USPACOM and the country team? Did this constitute a planning or design flaw?

# Bibliography


Abuza, Zachary, *Balik Terrorism: The Return of the Abu Sayyaf*, Carlisle, Pa.: Strategic Studies Institute, U.S. Army War College, September 2005. As of September 9, 2015:
http://www.strategicstudiesinstitute.army.mil/pubs/display.cfm?pubID=625

———, *The Philippines: Internal and External Security Challenges*, Australian Strategic Policy Institute Special Report 45, February 29, 2012. As of September 5, 2015:
https://www.aspi.org.au/publications/special-report-issue-45-the-philippines-internal-and-external-security-challenges

Adams, Jonathan, "In Basilan, Philippines, a US Counterterrorism Model Frays," *Christian Science Monitor*, December 11, 2008. As of September 5, 2015:
http://www.csmonitor.com/World/Asia-Pacific/2008/1211/p04s04-wosc.html

AFP—*See* Armed Forces of the Philippines.

Alipala, Julie S., "No Evidence of ISIS in Mindanao, Says US Envoy," *Inquirer*, November 14, 2014a. As of September 16, 2015:
http://globalnation.inquirer.net/114368/no-evidence-of-isis-in-mindanao-says-us-envoy

———, "3 Zamboanga City Siege Suspects Cry Torture," *Inquirer*, December 2, 2014b. As of September 16, 2015:
http://newsinfo.inquirer.net/654190/3-zamboanga-city-siege-suspects-cry-torture

Armed Forces of the Philippines, *Internal Peace and Security Plan, 'Bayanihan,'* Quezon City, Philippines, 2010. As of September 8, 2015:
http://www.army.mil.ph/pdf_files/bayanihan.pdf

Beaudette, Fran, *Philippine Counterinsurgency Success: Implications for the Human Domain of Warfare*, Carlisle Barracks, Pa.: U.S. Army War College, March 2013. As of September 5, 2015:
http://www.dtic.mil/cgi-bin/GetTRDoc?AD=ADA588594

"BIFF, Abu Sayyaf Pledge Allegiance to Islamic State Jihadists," Agence France-Presse, August 16, 2014.

Blair, Dennis C., "Commander's Guidance for Operation Freedom Eagle (OFE)," memorandum to Brig Gen Donald C. Wurster, commander, Joint Task Force 510, February 2, 2002.

Bodnar, Seth, and Jeremy Gwinn, "'Monetary Ammunition' in a Counterinsurgency," *Parameters*, Autumn 2010, pp. 1–12. As of October 7, 2015: http://www.dtic.mil/cgi-bin/GetTRDoc?AD=ADA538560

Boot, Max, and Richard Bennet, "Treading Softly in the Philippines: Why a Low-Intensity Counterinsurgency Strategy Seems to Be Working There," *Weekly Standard*, Vol. 14, No. 16, January 5, 2009. As of September 17, 2015: http://www.weeklystandard.com/Content/Public/Articles/000/000/015/956zznwj.asp

Bowden, Mark, "Jihadists in Paradise," *Atlantic*, March 1, 2007. As of December 28, 2014: http://www.theatlantic.com/magazine/archive/2007/03/jihadists-in-paradise/305613/

Briscoe, C. H., "Why the Philippines? ARSOF's Expanded Mission in the War on Terror," *Special Warfare*, Vol. 17, No. 1, September 2004a, pp. 2–11.

———, "Balikatan Exercise Spearheaded ARSOF Operations in the Philippines," *Special Warfare*, Vol. 17, No. 1, September 2004b, pp. 16–25.

Center for Army Lessons Learned, *Operation Enduring Freedom; Tactics, Techniques, and Procedures Handbook*, Fort Leavenworth, Kan., Handbook 02-8, June 2002. As of September 8, 2015: http://www.globalsecurity.org/military/library/report/call/call_02-8_toc.htm

Cho, Young M., Brady R. Clark, and Mark M. Lee, *Effective SOF Employment: Mitigating Causes of Conflict*, Monterey, Calif.: Naval Postgraduate School, thesis, June 2013. As of September 5, 2015: https://calhoun.nps.edu/handle/10945/34644

Comer, Richard, "Operation Enduring Freedom—Philippines (OEF-P)," *Defense Media Network*, August 23, 2012. As of February 12, 2015: http://www.defensemedianetwork.com/stories/winning-operation-enduring-freedom-philippines/

Crossman, Edgar G., "American–Philippine Relations: The Prospect," *Proceedings of the Academy of Political Science*, Vol. 22, No. 4, January 1948, pp. 25–36.

Daniels, Herb, *Keeping COIN Simple: The Outhouse Strategy for Security Development*, Special Operations Essays, 2009. As of September 5, 2015: https://calhoun.nps.edu/handle/10945/34385

Devesa, Roy, *An Assessment of the Philippine Counterinsurgency Operational Mythology*," Fort Leavenworth, Kan.: U.S. Army Command and General Staff College, thesis, June 17, 2005. As of September 5, 2015: http://www.dtic.mil/cgi-bin/GetTRDoc?AD=ADA441882

DoD—*See* U.S. Department of Defense.

Dunigan, Molly, Dick Hoffmann, Peter Chalk, Brian Nichiporuk, and Paul DeLuca, *Characterizing and Exploring the Implications of Maritime Irregular Warfare*, Santa Monica, Calif.: RAND Corporation, MG-1127-NAVY, 2012. As of September 5, 2015:
http://www.rand.org/pubs/monographs/MG1127.html

Empirical Studies of Conflict, "Philippines Overview," undated; referenced February 18, 2015. As of September 5, 2015:
http://esoc.princeton.edu/country/philippines

Farris, Stuart L., *Joint Special Operations Task Force—Philippines*, Fort Leavenworth, Kan.: School of Advanced Military Studies, U.S. Army Command and General Staff College, monograph, May 21, 2009. As of September 5, 2015:
http://handle.dtic.mil/100.2/ADA505075

Feickert, Andrew, *U.S. Military Operations in the Global War on Terrorism: Afghanistan, Africa, the Philippines, and Colombia*, Washington, D.C.: Congressional Research Service, Report for Congress, August 26, 2005. As of September 5, 2015:
http://oai.dtic.mil/oai/
oai?verb=getRecord&metadataPrefix=html&identifier=ADA458286

Felter, Joseph H., *Taking Guns to a Knife Fight: Effective Military Support to COIN*, Carlisle Barracks, Pa.: U.S. Army War College, thesis, April 1, 2009. As of September 5, 2015:
http://www.dtic.mil/cgi-bin/GetTRDoc?AD=ADA510853

Fowler, Mike, "Philippine Counterinsurgency Strategy: Then and Now," *Small Wars Journal*, January 18, 2011. As of September 5, 2015:
http://smallwarsjournal.com/blog/journal/docs-temp/651-fowler.pdf

Fridovich, David P., and Fred T. Krawchuk, "Winning in the Pacific: The Special Operation Forces Indirect Approach," *Joint Force Quarterly*, Issue 44, 1st Quarter, 2007. As of September 5, 2015:
http://www.dtic.mil/cgi-bin/GetTRDoc?AD=ADA481186

Gomez, Jim, "US Ends Philippines in Anti-Terror Force," Associated Press, June 26, 2014.

Gomlak, Matthew J., and Stephen Fenton. "Real Results: Military Partnerships in the Philippines," *Special Warfare*, Vol. 25, No. 3, July–September 2012. As of February 13, 2015:
http://www.soc.mil/swcs/SWmag/archive/SW2503/SW2503RealResults.html

Government of the Philippines and MILF—*See* Government of the Philippines and Moro Islamic Liberation Front.

Government of the Philippines and Moro Islamic Liberation Front, "Comprehensive Agreement on the Bangsamoro," March 27, 2014. As of September 16, 2015:
http://www.gov.ph/2014/03/27/document-cab/

Government of the Republic of the Philippines and Government of the United States of America, "Agreement Between the Government of the Republic of the Philippines and the Government of the United States of America on Enhanced Defense Cooperation," April 28, 2014. As of September 8, 2015:
http://www.gov.ph/2014/04/29/
document-enhanced-defense-cooperation-agreement/

GRP and United States—*See* Government of the Republic of the Philippines and Government of the United States of America.

Hall, Rosalie Arcala, "Boots on Unstable Ground: Democratic Governance of the Armed Forces Under Post 9/11 US-Philippine Military Relations," *Asia–Pacific Social Science Review*, Vol. 10, No. 2, 2010, pp. 25–42. As of September 5, 2015:
http://ejournals.ph/index.php?journal=dlsu-apssr&page=article&op=viewArticle&
path%5B%5D=1701

Hastings, Jonathan P., and Krishnamurti Mortela, *The Strategy–Legitimacy Paradigm: Getting It Right in the Philippines*, Monterey, Calif.: Naval Postgraduate School, thesis, December 2008. As of September 5, 2015:
http://www.dtic.mil/dtic/tr/fulltext/u2/a493812.pdf

Headquarters, Department of the Army, *Counterinsurgency*, Washington, D.C., Field Manual 3-24, Marine Corps Warfighting Publication 3-33.5, December 2006. As of September 12, 2015:
http://usacac.army.mil/cac2/Repository/Materials/COIN-FM3-24.pdf

Headquarters, Philippine Army, *Army Transformation Roadmap 2028 (Philippine Army's 18-Year Strategic Plan): A Journey Towards Good Governance and Performance Excellence*, Fort Andres Bonifacio, Manila, undated. As of September 15, 2015:
http://www.army.mil.ph/ATR2028.pdf

Headquarters, WestMinCom—*See* Headquarters, Western Mindanao Command.

Headquarters, Western Mindanao Command, "Campaign Assessment," briefing slides, undated.

Hendren, John, and Richard C. Paddock, "U.S. Military Plan Shelved in Philippines," *Los Angeles Times*, March 1, 2003. As of September 12, 2015:
http://articles.latimes.com/2003/mar/01/world/fg-phil1

Holt, Blaine D., "America in 3D: Has U.S. Foreign Policy Found Its Rebirth in the Philippines?" *American Foreign Policy Interests*, Vol. 33, No. 3, 2011, pp. 119–128.

HQ, Department of the Army—*See* Headquarters, Department of the Army.

HQ, PA—*See* Headquarters, Philippine Army.

Human Development Network, *Philippine Human Development Report 2005*, 2nd ed., 2005. As of September 9, 2015:
http://hdn.org.ph/2005-philippine-human-development-report-peace-human-security-and-human-development/

Human Rights Watch, "Philippines: Investigate Zamboanga Detainee Mistreatment," October 3, 2013. As of September 16, 2015:
https://www.hrw.org/news/2013/10/03/philippines-investigate-zamboanga-detainee-mistreatment

———, "World Report 2014: Philippines—Events of 2013," 2014. As of September 16, 2015:
http://www.hrw.org/world-report/2014/country-chapters/philippines

International Crisis Group, *The Philippines: Counter-Insurgency vs. Counter-Terrorism in Mindanao*, Asia Report 152, May 14, 2008. As of September 8, 2015:
http://www.crisisgroup.org/en/regions/asia/south-east-asia/philippines/152-the-philippines-counter-insurgency-vs-counter-terrorism-in-mindanao.aspx

———, *The Philippines: Local Politics in the Sulu Archipelago and the Peace Process*, Asia Report 225, May 2012. As of September 8, 2015:
http://www.crisisgroup.org/en/regions/asia/south-east-asia/philippines/225-the-philippines-local-politics-in-the-sulu-archipelago-and-the-peace-process.aspx

Interviews 1–78, conducted between August 13, 2013, and December 19, 2014. Numerous interviews were conducted with multiple interviewees.

Joint Special Operations Task Force—Philippines, "Joint Special Operations Task Force—Philippines: Operation Ultimatum," briefing slides, undated (a).

———, "JSOTF-P Security Assistance Update Brief for Secretary Reyes," briefing slides prepared for the Philippine secretary of defense, undated (b).

———, "JSOTF-P OPORD Information Paper," October 13, 2002.

———, "JSOTF-P Command Briefing," September 1, 2007a.

———, "Joint Special Operations Task Force—Philippines Methodology Briefing," briefing slides, September 2, 2007b.

———, "Joint Special Operations Task Force—Philippines Fact Sheet," February 2008a.

———, *Joint Special Operations Task Force—Philippines*, overview briefing, version 2, February 2008b. As of September 15, 2015:
http://www2.warwick.ac.uk/fac/soc/pais/people/aldrich/vigilant/powerpoints/JSOTF-P_overview_brief_feb_2008_ver_2.ppt

Joint Task Force 510, "JTF-510 Enduring Freedom-RP," briefing slides, undated.

JSOTF-P—*See* Joint Special Operations Task Force—Philippines.

Keating, Timothy J., *U.S. Pacific Command Posture*, statement before the Senate Armed Services Committee, March 19, 2009. As of February 13, 2015: http://www.alu.army.mil/ALU_INTERNAT/CountryNotes/PACOM/2.PACOM%20Posture%20Statement.pdf

Kenyon, Henry S., "Regional Partnerships Strengthen Pacific Operations," *SIGNAL*, October 2003. As of February 13, 2015: http://www.afcea.org/content/?q=node/72

Kowalewski, David, "Counterinsurgent Paramilitarism: A Philippine Case Study," *Journal of Peace Research*, Vol. 29, No. 1, February 1992, pp. 71–84.

Lambert, Geoffrey, Larry Lewis, and Sarah Sewall, "Operation Enduring Freedom—Philippines: Civilian Harm and the Indirect Approach," *Prism*, Vol. 3, No. 4, 2012, pp. 117–135.

Lastimado, Antonio R., and Arturo G. Rojas, *The Armed Force of the Philippines and Special Operations*, Monterey, Calif.: Naval Postgraduate School, thesis, December 2004. As of September 8, 2015: http://www.dtic.mil/dtic/tr/fulltext/u2/a429856.pdf

*Lim v. Arroyo*, G.R. 151445, April 11, 2002. As of September 11, 2015: http://sc.judiciary.gov.ph/jurisprudence/2002/apr2002/151445.htm

Lowery, William E., *Combating Terrorism in the Philippines to Improve U.S. Homeland Security*, Monterey, Calif.: Naval Postgraduate School, thesis, December 2010. As of September 8, 2015: http://www.dtic.mil/dtic/tr/fulltext/u2/a536052.pdf

Lum, Thomas, and Ben Dolven, *The Republic of the Philippines and U.S. Interests—2014*, Washington, D.C.: Congressional Research Service, R43498, May 15, 2014. As of September 17, 2015: https://www.fas.org/sgp/crs/row/R43498.pdf

Malone, Scott J., II, "Operation ULTIMATUM, Counterinsurgency Through, by, and with Host Nation Partners," Newport, R.I.: Naval War College, mimeograph, October 2007.

Marcelo, Elizabeth, "MILF Chair Iqbal: Bangsamoro Entity Still on Schedule," *GMA News Online*, November 28, 2014. As of September 8, 2015: http://www.gmanetwork.com/news/story/390263/news/nation/milf-chair-iqbal-bangsamoro-entity-still-on-schedule

Maxwell, David, "Commander's Summary of the Joint Special Operation Task Force Philippines (JSOTF-P) 2006–2007," report, undated (a).

———, "Commander's Summary of the Joint Special Operation Task Force Philippines (JSOTF-P) 2006–2007," summary, undated (b).

———, "Commander's Summary of Operations: Operation Enduring Freedom—Philippines," May 5, 2002.

———, "Foreign Internal Defense: An Indirect Approach to Counter-Insurgency/Counter Terrorism, Lessons from Operation Enduring Freedom—Philippines for Dealing with Non-Existential Threats to the United States," paper presented at conference of the Foreign Policy Research Institute, Washington, D.C., National Press Club, 2011.

Medina, Andrei, "Timeline: Crisis in Zamboanga City," *GMA News Online*, September 10, 2013. As of September 8, 2015:
http://www.gmanetwork.com/news/story/325855/news/regions/timeline-crisis-in-zamboanga-city

Narcise, Samuel, *Republic of the Philippines–United States of America Visiting Forces Agreement: Balikatan Exercises*, Carlisle Barracks, Pa.: U.S. Army War College, April 7, 2003. As of September 8, 2015:
http://www.dtic.mil/cgi-bin/GetTRDoc?AD=ADA414512

National Disaster Risk Reduction and Management Council, "Updates re the Effects of Typhoon 'Yolanda' (Haiyan)," Quezon City, Philippines, April 17, 2014. As of September 8, 2015:
http://www.ndrrmc.gov.ph/attachments/article/1329/Update_on_Effects_Typhoon_YOLANDA_(Haiyan)_17APR2014.pdf

Niksch, Larry, *Abu Sayyaf: Target of Philippine-U.S. Anti-Terrorism Cooperation*, Washington, D.C.: Congressional Research Service Report for Congress RL31265, January 24, 2007. As of September 8, 2015:
http://oai.dtic.mil/oai/oai?verb=getRecord&metadataPrefix=html&identifier=ADA463896

Oakley, Richard, "Operation Enduring Freedom Philippines: FID Success and the Way Forward," *Special Warfare*, Vol. 27, No. 1, January–March 2014, pp. 46–51. As of September 8, 2015:
http://www.soc.mil/swcs/SWmag/archive/SW2701/JAN-MAR_2013web.pdf

PAF LCE—*See* Philippine Air Force Liaison Coordination Element.

Palilonis, David C., *Operation Enduring Freedom—Philippines: A Demonstration of Economy of Force*, Newport, R.I.: Naval War College, May 4, 2009. As of September 8, 2015:
http://www.dtic.mil/cgi-bin/GetTRDoc?AD=ADA503066

"Partnered Counterterrorism Operations in the Philippines: A Case Study," Suffolk, Va.: Joint and Coalition Operational Analysis, August 30, 2011.

Peña, Leonardo I., *Finding the Missing Link to a Successful Philippine Counterinsurgency Strategy*, Monterey, Calif.: Naval Postgraduate School, thesis, June 2007. As of September 8, 2015:
https://calhoun.nps.edu/handle/10945/3393

Pew Research Center, *Global Opposition to U.S. Surveillance and Drones, but Limited Harm to America's Image*, Washington, D.C., July 2014. As of September 17, 2015:
http://www.pewglobal.org/2014/07/14/global-opposition-to-u-s-surveillance-and-drones-but-limited-harm-to-americas-image/

Philippine Air Force Liaison Coordination Element, "Mission Brief," briefing slides, October 12, 2012.

"Philippines Using US Smart Bombs," Associated Press, March 21, 2012.

"Policy Paralysis and Delays to Bangsamoro Basic Law Likely After Fighting Between Police and Militants in Philippines," *IHS Jane's 360*, February 12, 2015. As of October 7, 2015:
http://www.janes.com/article/48968/policy-paralysis-and-delays-to-bangsamoro-basic-law-likely-after-fighting-between-police-and-militants-in-philippines

Public Law 109-163, National Defense Authorization Act for Fiscal Year 2006, January 6, 2006. As of September 15, 2015:
http://www.gpo.gov/fdsys/pkg/PLAW-109publ163/content-detail.html

Quimpo, Nathan Gilbert, "The U.S. and the Southern Philippines' Quagmire," Asia Research Centre Working Paper 144, July 2007.

Radics, George Baylon, "Terrorism in Southeast Asia: Balikatan Exercises in the Philippines and the US 'War Against Terrorism,'" *Stanford Journal of East Asian Affairs*, Vol. 4, No. 2, May 21, 2004, pp. 115–127. As of September 8, 2015:
http://web.stanford.edu/group/sjeaa/journal42/seasia1.pdf

Rothstein, Hy S., "Less Is More: The Problematic Future of Irregular Warfare in an Era of Collapsing States," *Third World Quarterly*, Vol. 28, No. 2, 2007, pp. 275–294.

Scanzillo, Thomas M., *Influence: Maximizing Effects to Create Long-Term Stability*, Newport, R.I.: Naval War College, May 3, 2010. As of September 8, 2015:
http://www.dtic.mil/dtic/tr/fulltext/u2/a538741.pdf

Sepp, Kalev I., "Preparing for 2010: Thinking Outside the Box," *Special Warfare*, Vol. 10, No. 1, Winter 1997, pp. 2–6.

Serafino, Nina M., *Security Assistance Reform: "Section 1206" Background and Issues for Congress*, Washington, D.C.: Congressional Research Service, RS22855, April 19, 2013. As of September 15, 2015:
http://fpc.state.gov/documents/organization/209251.pdf

Sheehan, Michael A., *Crush the Cell: How to Defeat Terrorism Without Terrorizing Ourselves*, New York: Crown Publishers, 2008.

Simbulan, Roland G., "The Pentagon's Secret War and Facilities in the Philippines," *Peace Review*, Vol. 22, No. 2, 2010, pp. 150–157.

Special Inspector General for Afghanistan Reconstruction, "Governance and Development," undated. As of September 16, 2015: https://www.sigar.mil/quarterlyreports/fundingtables/governance-development.html

"Special Operations in PACOM," *Special Warfare*, Vol. 27, No. 1, January–March 2014. As of February 13, 2015: http://www.soc.mil/swcs/swmag/archive/SW2701/JAN-MAR_2013web.pdf

Stephan, Robert B., *Counterinsurgency in the Philippines: Problems and Prospects*, Langley Air Force Base, Va.: Army–Air Force Center for Low Intensity Conflict, October 1989. As of September 8, 2015: http://oai.dtic.mil/oai/oai?verb=getRecord&metadataPrefix=html&identifier=ADA226242

Swain, Richard, *Case Study: Operation Enduring Freedom Philippines*, U.S. Army Counterinsurgency Center, October 2010. As of September 8, 2015: http://www.dtic.mil/dtic/tr/fulltext/u2/a532988.pdf

Teutsch, Christian, and Sarah Thambidurai, "Southern Philippines Public Perception Survey," briefing to Special Operations Command, Pacific, staff, wave 7 findings, July 31, 2014.

Thayer, Carl, "Analyzing the US-Philippines Enhanced Defense Cooperation Agreement," *Diplomat*, May 2, 2014. As of February 12, 2015: http://thediplomat.com/2014/05/analyzing-the-us-philippines-enhanced-defense-cooperation-agreement/

TNS Qualitative, "Insights into Filipinos in Mindanao: Qualitative Research Findings for Project Achilles Wave 8," September 2014.

U.S. Agency for International Development, *Performance Evaluation of USAID/Philippines Growth with Equity in Mindanao III (GEM-3) Program: Annexes*, undated. As of September 8, 2015: https://www.usaid.gov/sites/default/files/documents/1861/SIs_Final_Evaluation_Report-Growth_Equity_Mindanao_III_Annexes.pdf

———, *U.S. Overseas Loans and Grants: Obligations and Loan Authorizations July 1, 1945–September 30, 2013*, CONG-R-0105, 2015. As of October 7, 2015: https://explorer.usaid.gov/reports-greenbook.html

USAID—*See* U.S. Agency for International Development.

U.S. Code, Title 22, Foreign Relations and Intercourse, Chapter 22, Mutual Security Assistance.

U.S. Department of Defense, *Department of Defense Section 1209 and Section 1203(b) Report to Congress on Foreign-Assistance Related Programs for Fiscal Years 2008, 2009, and 2010*, April 2012a. As of September 15, 2015: http://securityassistance.org/sites/default/files/1204_1209_rept.pdf

———, *Department of Defense Section 1209 and Section 1203(b) Report to Congress on Foreign-Assistance Related Programs for Fiscal Year 2011*, October 2012b. As of September 15, 2015:
http://www.dod.gov/pubs/foi/Reading_Room/Other/14-F-0197_DOC_01_Department_of_Defense_Section_1209_and_Section_1203b_report_to_congress_FY11.pdf

U.S. Department of State, "Background Information on Terrorist Groups," *Patterns of Global Terrorism*, April 30, 2001. As of September 8, 2015:
http://www.state.gov/j/ct/rls/crt/2000/2450.htm

———, "Country Reports on Terrorism 2013," April 2014. As of September 8, 2015:
http://www.state.gov/j/ct/rls/crt/2013/

U.S. Joint Chiefs of Staff, *Foreign Internal Defense*, Joint Publication 3-22, July 12, 2010. As of September 9, 2015:
http://www.dtic.mil/doctrine/new_pubs/jp3_22.pdf

———, *Department of Defense Dictionary of Military and Associated Terms*, Joint Publication 1-02, November 8, 2010, as amended through June 15, 2015. As of September 8, 2015:
http://www.dtic.mil/doctrine/dod_dictionary

Watts, Stephen, Jason H. Campbell, Patrick B. Johnston, Sameer Lalwani, and Sarah H. Bana, *Countering Others' Insurgencies: Understanding U.S. Small-Footprint Interventions in Local Context*, Santa Monica, Calif.: RAND Corporation, RR-513-SRF, 2014. As of September 8, 2015:
http://www.rand.org/pubs/research_reports/RR513.html

Wilson, Gregory, "Anatomy of a Successful COIN Operation: OEF-Philippines and the Indirect Approach," *Military Review*, Vol. 86, No. 6, November–December 2006, pp. 38–48. As of September 8, 2015:
http://usacac.army.mil/CAC2/MilitaryReview/Archives/English/MilitaryReview_2008CRII0831_art009.pdf

Wurster, Donald, "JTF-510—Enduring Freedom-RP," briefing slides, undated.

———, letter addressed to ADM Dennis Blair, February 2002.